THE POWER OF THE TEXAS GOVERNOR
CONNALLY TO BUSH

The Power
of the Texas
Governor

CONNALLY TO BUSH

by Brian McCall
Foreword by William P. Hobby, Jr.

UNIVERSITY OF TEXAS PRESS   AUSTIN

*The publication of this book was supported by
the Jess and Betty Jo Hay Endowment.*

Requests for permission to reproduce material
from this work should be sent to:
> Permissions
> University of Texas Press
> P.O. Box 7819
> Austin, TX 78713-7819
> utpress.utexas.edu/index.php/rp-form

♾ The paper used in this book meets the minimum requirements
of ANSI/NISO Z39.48-1992 (R1997) (Permanence of Paper).

LIBRARY OF CONGRESS CATALOGING-IN-PUBLICATION DATA

McCall, Brian, 1958–
   The power of the Texas governor : Connally to Bush / by Brian McCall ;
foreword by William P. Hobby, Jr. — 1st ed.
      p. cm.
   Includes bibliographical references and
   index. I SBN 978- 1- 4773- 1018- 2
      1. Governors—Texas—History—20th century. 2. Governors—Texas—
Biography. 3. Texas—Politics and government—1951– 4. Political leadership—
Texas—Case studies. 5. Executive power—Texas—Case studies. I. Title.
   F391.2.M22 2009
   976.4'0630922—dc22
                                                      2008027033

For Nellie Hutchins McCall and David Benjamin McCall, Jr.,
Who gave me everything . . .
With love and gratitude

CONTENTS

Foreword   ix

Acknowledgments   xi

1 GOVERNANCE   1

2 JOHN CONNALLY   9

3 PRESTON SMITH   21

4 DOLPH BRISCOE   33

5 WILLIAM P. CLEMENTS   45

6 MARK WHITE   61

7 WILLIAM P. CLEMENTS'S SECOND TERM   79

8 ANN RICHARDS   89

9 GEORGE W. BUSH   113

10 CONCLUSION   129

Notes   141

Bibliography   151

Index   157

FOREWORD

TEXAS STATE government is one of the businesses I grew up in. I have known several Texas governors. My father was the best. Both my grandfathers were legislators. As parliamentarian and later president of the Texas Senate (lieutenant governor) for eighteen years, I've seen how they work.

The governor does not run the highway system or the prisons or the universities. But in four or eight years he (or she) appoints thousands of board members who oversee the scores of state agencies that educate, police, and provide human services. Those board members serve six-year terms, many of those years coming after the appointing governor has gone.

The Texas governor has a long footprint. Through his or her appointees, a governor instills a philosophy into the workings of those institutions.

In this book, Brian McCall gives a fresh look at the power, prowess, personality, and punch that a governor can bring to the office and the process. He documents his observations with well-chosen anecdotes. After the election is over, the hard work starts.

Within constitutional limits, the power of the office is as big as the governor wills it to be.

William P. Hobby, Jr.

ACKNOWLEDGMENTS

I WISH to thank those who consented to be interviewed for this book. In addition, my thanks go to Libby Goss for transcribing the tapes of those interviews. I also thank Oren Lund for his help with research, and Wilfrid Koponen and Kip Keller for copyediting the manuscript.

I would like most especially to thank Dennis and Abby Kratz for initially suggesting this project, and Anthony Champagne, whose guidance made this a better work than it otherwise would have been. And special thanks to Bill Bishel, Katie Jones, Victoria Davis, and the good people at the University of Texas Press. Special gratitude and respect is extended to Paul Burka and Carolyn Barta for their most insightful observations.

Finally, I am grateful for those who have knocked me down in life, and those who have helped me get back up.

*You cannot play with the animal in you without becoming
wholly animal, play with falsehood without forfeiting
your right to truth, play with cruelty without losing your
sensitivity of mind. He who wants to keep his garden tidy
doesn't reserve a plot for weeds.*

DAG HAMMARSKJÖLD, *Markings*

THE POWER OF THE TEXAS GOVERNOR
CONNALLY TO BUSH

1

GOVERNANCE

IN THE PAST five centuries, under several forms of government, Texas has been governed by eighty-nine governors, a presidial captain, and four presidents. Ninety-four men and two women have directed the government of Texas under six flags—as a province, a republic, and a state. This is an examination of politics and the use of power in the modern governorship of the last four decades: the administrations of Governor John Connally through Governor George W. Bush.

When John Connally became governor, Texas had a population of fewer than ten million people. When George W. Bush assumed the governorship, there were approximately nineteen million Texans. Connally's first legislative appropriation was less than three billion dollars, while Bush's first state budget exceeded seventy-eight billion dollars. To be sure, the state changed dramatically in many ways during that time, from a rural, agricultural, and oil-based economy to a diverse, high-technology economy driven more by powerful brains than brawny backs. Along with those changes came adaptations in governance.

It is widely reported that the governorship of Texas is by design a weak office. However, the strength of an individual governor's personality can overcome many of the limitations imposed on the office. Capitol observer Paul Burka writes: "The fundamentals of governing are candor, competence, loyalty, and leadership. This is true during booms and busts, for Republicans and Democrats, in times of ideological fervor and in times of pragmatism. Personality transcends policy."[1]

There is no better laboratory for studying human behavior than the Texas Capitol. Because gubernatorial powers in Texas are not specifically enumerated, observing the use of those powers can be instructive. A strong governor has a strong will and understands how to mobilize the wills of others effectively.

Texas generally elects colorful people to the post. Writing on leadership, Richard Nixon observes that to be effective, leaders must touch people emotionally: "The politician, no less than the actor or the filmmaker, knows that to bore his audience is to lose his audience.

Thus, few great political leaders are dull. They cannot afford to be. Political leadership has to appeal to the head, but it must also appeal to the heart."[2] Texans vote with both head and heart. Challengers who have new messages can defeat popular governors—hence Bush's victory over Ann Richards. Smart, successful candidates with agendas perfectly in line with the desires of the majority of voters, but who fail to make an emotional connection with voters, lose to more empathetic challengers whose views are less familiar—hence Richards's defeat of Clayton Williams. In fact, Williams failed so signally to connect with the voting public, despite his solid campaign, that it was said he would "win the governorship—unless he goes door-to-door!"

The most powerful person in any relationship is the most flexible one. This is particularly true in gubernatorial leadership. Effective leaders must weigh the need to achieve important goals against the necessity of resorting to unpalatable ways of achieving them. Winston Churchill once remarked of a nineteenth-century leader who failed to reach his potential that "he would not stoop; he did not conquer."

Humility, one could argue, is the mother's milk of politics. It could also be said that whom God wishes to strike down, God first gives political success. Hard-fought legislative victories often come at a governor's moment of greatest peril. Legislators are pressed, and promises are made during long periods of give-and-take. Napoleon said, "The greatest dangers occur at the time of victory." Members of the legislative branch enjoy their power and are not reluctant to exercise it to the detriment of a governor whom they believe to be ungrateful or haughty. A governor must pay attention to all legislators. An appointee of what one senator felt to be an aloof John Connally lost Senate confirmation by one vote. The senator who cast the deciding vote explained that he did so "just to let the governor know I exist."[3]

Just as important as knowing what to do as governor is to know what *not* to do. A governor must have the will to stay out of other people's fights and to avoid getting dragged into strategically unimportant battles. The governor must judge struggles by what they will yield and what they will cost. Nietzsche wrote: "The value of a thing sometimes lies not in what one attains with it, but in what one pays for it—what it *costs* us." The governor must ask not only, "Can I attain the goal?" but also, even of a worthy goal, "At what price?"

Mary Beth Rogers, chief of staff to Governor Ann Richards, says that an effective governor focuses on two or three key goals and commits all resources to them instead of getting spread too thin. At the beginning of Richards's governorship, this approach worked. As Rogers notes, "I feel really good about our first few months in office because we stuck to our plan, and things just rolled on through. We knew what we were supposed to do, and we all did it. I think that's important."[4] However, establishing momentum and maintaining it are different issues. As Rogers puts it, "I think any leader over time wears down, and the staff in particular wears down. You need to be rejuvenated, reenergized, and I think that is difficult to do."[5] Part of the problem, especially for a governor who loses focus, is the limits on the governor's powers: "When you couldn't dominate the legislature, you were limited in your ability to get anything done. That became a problem. It's a structural flaw in Texas government."[6]

However, a resourceful governor can overcome these flaws. When asked about the built-in limitation in gubernatorial authority in Texas, Governor Mark White quoted Allan Shivers, whom White called "one of my favorites." As White explained, Shivers said, "when asked about the weak governorship in Texas, 'I *never* thought it was weak. I had all the power I needed.'"[7] Writing retrospectively about the powers of the governor after seven and a half years in office, Shivers remarked:

> No special session of the Legislature will be called except by him. No convict will be pardoned or paroled unless he approves. No man or woman will be appointed to a state board, no vacancies in office filled, and no special elections called except at his direction. He cannot be forced to act, even by the courts, as the Texas Constitution exempts him from *mandamus* and *quo warranto* proceedings. Martial law will not be declared unless he declares it. The militia will not be called out unless he calls it. Only he can veto legislative acts, sign proclamations, and permit fugitives to be extradited. These are ordinary, almost routine, prerogatives of the governor.[8]

Through the traditional State of the State address given at the beginning of each regular legislative session, the governor has an opportunity to outline legislative priorities and to persuade legislators and others of their importance. This bully pulpit gives the governor an excellent opportunity to cause the various stakeholders to focus on his initiatives. From there, effective governors mobilize interest groups, select floor sponsors, meet with key legislators to elicit support, work with business and public policy leaders, and meet with editorial boards and party leaders.

If a governor's program is not fulfilled to the governor's satisfaction during a regular legislative session, the governor can call and set the agendas for an unlimited number of thirty-day special sessions concerned only with the governor's specific requests.

Because Texas legislators serve part-time in a job that pays less than the cost to serve, most maintain full-time careers in addition to holding political office. Therefore, often the mere threat by a governor to call a special session can advance the governor's cause or add to a bill's vote tally. Once a special session begins, a governor can add items to the legislative agenda—a useful bargaining chip, since legislators' pet bills can be included in exchange for their support of the governor's program.

The governor of Texas can veto any piece of legislation for any reason—or without a reason—and has the power of the line-item veto for specific appropriations in the state budget. In short, the governor can eliminate spending on certain items without vetoing an entire appropriations bill. Likewise, the governor can strike spending for various things deemed important by the legislature without giving an explanation; the governor can do this for political reasons. However, the governor may not reduce the spending in any budget item; rather, the governor must strike out the entire budget line or let it stand. Skilled legislators can design budget lines to make it politically difficult for the governor to veto the item. The threat of a veto can prompt lawmakers to modify their bills to be more palatable to the governor, or even to cause lawmakers to "pull them down."

The governor can grant clemency to convicted criminals. Typically, the governor acts on the advice of the governor-appointed Pardons and Paroles Board. On the recommendation of the board, the governor can grant a criminal a full pardon or a conditional pardon, or can commute a death sentence to a sentence of life in prison.

On his own, a governor can grant a thirty-day stay of execution in a capital case. Things in Texas were not always so formal. Indeed, this layer of protection was set to buffer governors' actions. Governor James "Pa" Ferguson was quick to pardon, and a convict once escaped from the prison in Huntsville so that he could call Ferguson and ask for a pardon. Ferguson lectured the man about the wrongness of having escaped. Nevertheless, the governor promised to pardon the man eventually, provided that he return to prison on his own and serve the remainder of his sentence. The governor "then wrote a 'To Whom it May Concern' letter identifying the man and saying that he was returning to prison. The man, unaccompanied, returned as promised, and when he had completed his sentence, he received a pardon, sent via telegram to him at Huntsville."[9] The restriction limiting the governor's discretionary power to a thirty-day stay of execution reflects a more modern sensibility.

Perhaps the most significant executive power is the ability to appoint individuals to governmental positions. Every governor has the opportunity to appoint approximately two thousand individuals to boards and commissions and to fill vacancies in nonlegislative offices. Nevertheless, this power is limited by the fact that all of the governor's appointments must by ratified by a two-thirds vote of the Senate—as opposed to the simple-majority approval of U.S. presidential appointments. Because most board and commission members serve overlapping terms, usually for six years, a governor is able to fill about one-third of all positions every two years.

The Texas Constitution names the governor as "commander-in-chief of the military force of the State, except when they are called into actual service of the United States."[10] As such, the governor can mobilize the Texas National Guard during riots or natural disasters to safeguard citizens' lives, property, and security.

Texas governors who enjoyed the most success had high aims, ones that they articulated clearly, as well as patience in deliberation, a sense of balance, firmness, ability, and principle. They rose to the occasion, and, often, they created those occasions. They dealt effectively with crises and emergencies. They hired and appointed reliable, capable people. They gave to the office more than they took from it. They exhibited courage and charm. They had a sense of history. They had an innate sense of knowing which battles were worthy of the fight and which were not. They understood that principles are eternal. Governors fail when they abandon these essential qualities of statesmanship. The worst not only fail to "honor the principles of statesmanship, but also they fail to recognize them, having failed to learn them, having failed to want to learn them."[11]

Formal examinations of the politics of leadership offer rich—and often contradictory—theories of the impact of the individual on the gubernatorial office. Perhaps this is because individual governors alter the character of gubernatorial power and uniquely mark it. In his classic examination of the politics of presidential leadership, Richard Neustadt looked at the human qualities that a president brings to the job, namely: a sense of purpose, a feel for power, and a source of confidence.[12] These and the other personal characteristics mentioned above are particularly worth examining when studying leadership among Texas governors. In areas where formal powers are shared, governors must rely upon informal powers in order to succeed.

2

JOHN CONNALLY

*In November 1962, using his secret taping system . . .
[President Kennedy] had called to congratulate Connally on
his election.*

*In this overlooked recording, the governor-elect reports
that a Republican "hate campaign" in Dallas generated a
"hell of a protest vote" against "you and the vice-president
and me."*

*JFK asks, "What did we lose Dallas by—do you
remember—in '60?"*

"Yes, sir, you lost by over sixty thousand votes."

*"Sixty thousand votes!" cries Kennedy. "You know, they're
up here talking to me—you remember—about having that
federal building down there."*

*Then, JFK speaks to the governor in language chilling to
hear in the afterknowledge of their doomed limousine ride
into the city.*

*"I don't know why we do anything for Dallas. I'm telling
you—they just murdered all of us!"*

MICHAEL BESCHLOSS, *Presidential Courage*

LBJ said that John Connally was not comfortable unless he was in a three-hundred-dollar suit and in the company of men wearing three-hundred-dollar suits.

JOHN CONNALLY changed the Texas governorship. Paul Burka describes Governor Connally as "nothing less than the architect of modern Texas. He understood his moment in history perfectly, and he seized it."[1] As secretary of the navy and a friend of both President Lyndon B. Johnson and President John F. Kennedy, Connally was the first modern Texas governor to be a national figure.[2] He arrived with the advent of television advertising, and that medium served him well. Connally knew and understood Texas politics, having been Lyndon Johnson's secretary, campaign manager, friend, and confidant since 1939. After a year in Washington as Kennedy's secretary of the navy, Connally, at age forty-three, was ready to come home and run for office himself for the first time.

Connally recalls that he made many acquaintances throughout the state while working in Johnson's senatorial campaigns in 1941 (unsuccessful) and 1948 (successful), something that was overlooked by many political observers at the time. Nonetheless, Connally notes, "There wasn't a [newspaper] publisher in the State of Texas that I hadn't known pretty well. There wasn't a one that I couldn't call on or go see. This doesn't mean they were all committed to me, but at least I had an entrée. I'd had some working relationship with nearly all the top editors and publishers in the State during those two statewide campaigns for Johnson."[3]

Where Connally had come from and where he would end up reflected a changing Texas. From a humble background as the son of a tenant farmer in rural Texas, he had benefited from a public school system and a public university system that challenged his keen mind. His good looks, memory for names, drive to succeed, and attractive personality allowed him to run successfully for student body president at the University of Texas. He married Idanell (Nellie) Brill, a campus beauty, and graduated from law school at the university. All the while, he added names to his Rolodex.

Connally made sure that he became connected politically to the highest degree, and he developed high-level business contacts. As a young attorney for the prominent Fort Worth millionaire Sid Richardson, Connally sat on the board of the New York Central Railway.

He negotiated the purchase of radio stations and drugstore chains. As a result, his political and business experiences outpaced those of much older men. He understood the inner workings of the public and private sectors at the very top. Political advisor Julian Read recalls an instance in which some businessmen tried to outmaneuver Connally. In response, Connally demonstrated his ability to sum up such circumstances with a colorful image: "They're not going to handle me that way. I've been upstairs, where they have the two-dollar beer!"[4]

Connally was aware of a small political consulting firm in Fort Worth run by Read. Read's firm had been primarily involved in local races, but had recently orchestrated the congressional election of Jim Wright over an incumbent congressman who was backed by the power structure and the *Fort Worth Star-Telegram*. Connally called Read and asked for a meeting at Fort Worth's Hotel Texas. Read says that Connally's call left a vivid impression. As secretary of the navy, Connally had learned that all the federal research grants were going to "California, New York, Connecticut—not Texas. Connally saw a whole new world in Washington and said, you know, Texas has to change. He said, 'If Texas is going to be part of the future for this country and the world, Texas needs to change from this agrarian economy of oil and gas, and the key to that is education.' That is what he spelled out to me, that was his vision for Texas, and that was the pitch. That became the backbone of our whole campaign."[5]

Although by then it was a formality, Connally invited a few men to be his guests at Dolph Briscoe's 165,000-acre Catarina Ranch to discuss his candidacy. In addition to Briscoe, others present were Frank Erwin, Democratic Party chair Will Davis, Representative Ben Barnes, Robert Strauss, Lloyd Bentsen, and Eugene Locke. According to Davis, this tactic of inviting people he knew to such events was one that Connally used to good effect throughout his years in public life. He would ask these trusted confidants "a particular question—in this case: what did they think of his opportunity to run for governor? He would listen very carefully to their advice and take it under consideration. If he could get a consensus from the group, he usually followed that consensus."[6] From there, the campaign began. Connally started his ten-month campaign in early 1962, before the other candidates did, telling audiences—in an attempt to dispel rumors that he was running at Johnson's behest—that the decision to run was "mine and mine alone. I sought the advice of many. I asked the permission of none. We should make up our minds, as I have made up mine, that we should be the strong state of this nation. Together, we can make Texas first in the nation in education, in industrial growth, in the broadening of job opportunities, and in the exercise of state responsibility to all people."[7]

Despite the fact that only 4 percent of Texans were for Connally at the outset of the campaign, he won the first primary ahead of liberal Don Yarborough by 113,512 votes, with incumbent governor Price Daniel in third place, Attorney General Will Wilson fourth, Texas highway commissioner Marshall Formby fifth, and right-wing Major General Edwin Walker in last place. Connally outspent Yarborough $493,462 to $231,863 and went on to win the runoff by 26,250 votes out of a total of 1,104,098 votes cast.

With the nomination won, Connally faced Republican candidate Jack Cox in November. Though previous Republican gubernatorial candidates had rarely garnered over 12 percent of the vote, Cox was different. He was a former Democrat and an attractive candidate. In an airplane campaign blitz that started in San Antonio and ended up in Corpus Christi, Connally swept into thirty-one cities in approximately forty-eight hours, beating Cox—by far the largest Republican gubernatorial vote getter up to that point—by only 132,000 votes. For the first time since Texas had become a state in 1845, all of the state's top elected officials were new: Governor Connally, Lieutenant Governor Preston Smith, Attorney General Waggoner Carr, and House Speaker Byron Tunnell.

The oil-rich Texas that Connally sought to direct ranked thirty-third in per capita income, near last in adult literacy, and last in spending for child-welfare services. There were more poor people in Texas than in any other state in the nation. In public education, the state ranked near the bottom; only 2 percent of blacks attended integrated schools.

In addressing both legislative houses in his first State of the State address in 1963, Connally hit hard on the very issues that he had discussed with political consultant Julian Read months earlier:

Unless our nation produces more and better brainpower, our system of democratic government, our personal liberties, will soon

perish. One need look only to the vast complexes of industry surrounding institutions such as MIT, California Tech, Johns Hop-
kins, and the University of Michigan for evidence of this. How
well are the institutions of higher education in Texas meeting
this challenge? A number of indices can help provide an answer.
One is the number of PhD degrees produced by educational institutions in the various states. In the academic year 1959–1960,
Texas produced 297 PhDs. In the same year, New York produced
1,145, California 949, and Massachusetts 784. The University of
California alone produced more PhDs than all of the public and
private institutions in Texas.[8]

This was anything but a merely academic matter to Connally or
Texas, for much more was involved than the prestige of the universities
cited. Producing highly trained people to work on research grants and
in high-tech industries had huge economic implications. As Connally
himself explained, "In the federal fiscal year 1961, California received
51.34% of the Defense Department budget for experimental and de-
velopmental test and research work and 23.9%—or $5.277 billion—
of prime defense contract awards. In federal fiscal year 1961, the State
of Utah received *three* times as much as the State of Texas in Defense
Department research contracts."[9]

Connally admonished legislators to look at faculty pay, pointing
out that average faculty salaries at the University of Texas ranked 46th
out of 124 similar institutions. Speaking of Texas institutions of higher
education, he said that their greatness depended not on the edifices
erected on university campuses, but upon "the inspiration, direction,
and leadership of great teachers." He noted, "There are not many
such teachers, for intellectual brilliance cannot be mass-produced.
We must keep such teachers in Texas and attract more. To do this, we
must match the competition of other states."[10] Toward that end, as an
emergency matter, he established the Governor's Committee on Education beyond the High School. His belief was that for Texas to lead
the nation and the world economically, an investment in brainpower
would require the commitment of influential people across the state.

According to Larry Temple, Connally's chief of staff, when Connally
stressed educational excellence and the importance of brainpower and

technology, he was raising an issue that everyone else in Texas was ignoring at the time. The issue was not trendy, and many people from business and public life he asked to serve on the committee refused his request. However, Connally persisted with a handful of individuals, and all of them "ultimately said yes because he wouldn't take no for an answer. He got the people who were opinion makers who could affect decisions in the business community, knowing that he was probably going to raise taxes to pay for the committee's recommendations. He knew what the committee was going to come up with. He knew what the facts were that they had to come up with. He helped feed them to do that."[11] Connally persuaded Henry Bartell (Pat) Zachry of San Antonio, the founder of the H. B. Zachry Company, to chair the committee, and persuaded Morgan Davis, the CEO of Humble Oil, and John Erik Jonsson, cofounder of Texas Instruments, to serve as members. Never before had such a panel been assembled. Previously, "You had the studies, but not with that muscle," observed Julian Read.[12]

Later, Connally formed a committee to work on improvements in public education. Ernie Stromberger, the AP capital correspondent, recalls that Connally drew enormous power from his influence within the business world of Texas and his association with Lyndon Johnson.[13] Stromberger elaborates,

> The other factor that was influential was that in the early
> '60s—compared to now—the economy of Texas was in the hands
> of Texans. All the banks were owned by Texans; all of the big
> insurance agencies were owned by Texans; a lot of the big oil
> producers were Texans; and, even the grocery stores and drug-
> stores were owned by Texans. And so a man like Connally could
> go to his experiences with Lyndon Johnson's fund-raising and the
> people who funded his campaigns and carry that cachet of being
> a part of the Johnson machine. He could reach into the business
> community and mobilize the local bankers and local business-
> men to do something good for Texas because these men had a
> stake in Texas. Well, now you don't have that.[14]

In addition, the Texas media at that time were owned by Texans. These things combined to make it possible for Connally to persuade the stakeholders needed to achieve his ambitious goals for higher education. To pay for his education proposals, Connally proposed a $32.9 million tax bill, and it passed the legislature, without changes, before the appropriations bill.

Connally wanted an extra $26 million for higher education, but Speaker Tunnell and Lieutenant Governor Smith cut that proposed budget number in half. After two days and nights of negotiations, Connally gave up, and the reduced appropriations bill handily passed. Mindful of the thirteen million dollars that had been sliced from his higher-education bill, Connally used the governor's line-item veto to cut $12,439,924 from the budget bill. He did so, as he said, to provide in effect "a substantial down payment on excellence in education. I intend to let it accumulate as a surplus to use for that purpose. And you may rest assured that I plan to guard that nest egg like an old mother hen."[15]

While his State of the State address in 1963 covered many other priorities—including equal rights for women and eradication of the screwworm—Connally focused on two other matters that overshadow most items that come before the legislature. As he put it, "Our action on these three vital issues, will, in my judgment, go far toward shaping the destiny of Texas for our children and for their children."[16]

The other two priorities were tourism and industrial development. He proposed a tourist-attraction program and requested an appropriation of a half million dollars for the biennium. Connally argued that everyone in Texas benefits from tourism, noting that tourists spent about $480 million in Texas in 1962, of which about $25 million went to the state in direct taxes. This, he felt, was ample evidence that a stepped-up program to attract tourism would pay many dividends. Later that year, a law created the Texas Tourist Development Agency. In addition, he called for the creation of the Office of Economic Development to strengthen the state's ability to attract jobs; its goal was to provide 800,000 new jobs in Texas by 1970. By the end of Connally's first year in office, the state had added 317 new plants and warehouses—second only to New York.[17] Connally was pleased with the results of his first legislative session.

On November 22, 1963, the assassin's bullets that killed the president of the United States also entered the governor's back and left through his chest, destroying a rib and leaving a gaping hole larger than a throat opening. On the way to Parkland Hospital, Connally lost about one-third of his blood. His survival was uncertain. The eyes of the world were on Dallas, as Connally's oldest and closest political ally was sworn in as president of the United States.

If ever there was doubt about Connally's reelection, those doubts had been erased by then. He was politically untouchable. With little support, Don Yarborough again challenged Connally, but was trounced in a large presidential-election-year turnout—1,125,884 to 471,411. Republicans put up a sacrificial lamb in Jack Crichton in the general election. Connally ran a mere token campaign, but overwhelmed the challenger.

The nation and the state focused on John Connally and admired his commanding, poised presence. Political journalist Richard Morehead described Connally as a man who "came closer to being a movie fan's idea of a leader than anybody I knew in public office: handsome, wavy-haired, tall, and articulate, with a high sense of drama."[18] Connally understood how to best play to these strengths, personally selecting as guards Texas Rangers who were two inches shorter than he was. He dressed impeccably in expensive suits, causing Lyndon Johnson to remark that Connally was not comfortable unless he was in a three-hundred-dollar suit and in the company of men wearing three-hundred-dollar suits. He rode in parades in cowboy outfits from Christian Dior. He both looked and acted the part of governor. When he walked into a room, he had the attention of everyone present. Former aide Nick Krajl recalls that rather than paying court to the powerful people, Connally would enter a room and walk over to "the person you thought was the least important in that room, like a child or somebody that was way down. He already *had* the people who were up the totem pole."[19]

However, perfect appearances can create envy that simmers within silent—or not so silent—enemies. Senator Babe Schwartz of Galveston recounts a debate on the Senate floor in which Senator Andy Rogers of Childress offended the absent governor. Rogers announced to the chamber that the governor must be "over there, getting his hair 'blued' at the beauty salon."[20] Some lawmakers felt slighted when they were unable to immediately see Governor Connally without an appointment, since they had been able to see previous governors with-

The elegant John and Nellie Connally, 1963.

out one. John Mobley, one of Connally's executive assistants, recalls that most legislators believed that Connally "didn't spend enough time with them. He'd say they were right, but he just had other ways of getting things done. He'd talk to their supporters. Mass communication. He knew people in their district, or his friends were their friends."[21]

As his second legislative session approached, Connally was still stinging from the loss of the thirteen million dollars in higher-education funds taken from him by the presiding officers of the two legislative houses. In a brilliant power move, Connally facilitated the election of his loyal friend, Ben Barnes, to the speakership by appointing Speaker Tunnell to the Railroad Commission. Connally effectively took control of the House of Representatives. Ben Barnes recalls that since John Connally did not like to "sit down and talk to members of the Legislature, I guess as speaker of the House, I probably sold Connally's programs more than he sold them."[22]

According to Larry Temple, Connally was uncomfortable with Tunnell's leadership in the House, even though he bore no animosity toward Tunnell—which was evident in the fact that Connally had appointed Tunnell to the Railroad Commission. Nonetheless, Connally wanted someone more progressive, "and Connally thought he wanted some things done in the Legislature in '65 that would require some spending, particularly in higher education, and some changes to be made that he thought likely would not have been made under the Byron Tunnell regime. So when the vacancy came along on the Railroad Commission, Connally thought it was a very fortuitous situation to open up the opportunity for Ben to be elected speaker."[23]

John Connally and Ben Barnes made an effective team. Connally laid out his goals for the next legislative session in the House chamber in January 1965. He was direct in his assessment of the State of the State and clear about the need to improve education in Texas. He used disappointing statistics to mobilize change: "13 of every 100 Texans over the age of 25 are functionally illiterate; only four of ten first graders graduate from high school, and fewer than half of our college freshman stay to earn their first degree. Despite massive efforts to upgrade our educational establishment between 1940 and 1960, Texas dropped from twentieth to twenty-ninth among the forty-eight continental states in the median number of school years completed by its citizens. Texas is not where it can be—nor where it ought to be—in educational quality."[24]

Accordingly, Connally proposed statutory adoption of the course defined by the Committee on Education beyond the High School, including the creation of the Higher Education Coordinating Board—a central board appointed by the governor to oversee college education in Texas. He also proposed the creation of the Fine Arts Commission, some public school reforms, and a reorganization of state water and mental health agencies. His recommended budget was $254 million higher than the previous budget. Again, the legislature went along with Connally, appropriating substantially more money for higher education and creating both the Higher Education Coordinating Board and the Fine Arts Commission. The legislature provided more funding for both his tourism and industrial-development interests and assisted in his efforts to improve water planning. It was another successful legislative session.

Despite having criticized his predecessor, Price Daniel, for seeking a fourth term, and despite having asked the legislature to limit governors to two terms, Connally sought a third term. His Democratic opponent, Stanley Woods, a forty-three-year-old Houston oilman with a law degree, referred to the governor as "King John." Running a slick campaign, Connally won with 74 percent of the vote. In the general election, Connally beat Republican T. E. Kennerly with 72 percent of the total vote.

Despite this impressive victory, Connally, by all accounts, became bored with the job during his third term. He disliked the ceremonial tasks that took up so much of his day, and grew tired of dealing with Lieutenant Governor Smith, with whom he had little in common and whom he did not respect. He challenged the legislature to pass a proposal for a convention to rewrite the state's bloated constitution. Although the legislature complied, the voters turned the measure down. Connally called for annual legislative sessions and a four-year term for all statewide elected officials, but neither became law. However, his popularity remained high, and his accomplishments were real.

Although few doubt that Connally could have sought and won a fourth term as governor, he was tired. More importantly, he had a political instinct that is rare among politicians: he knew when to get off the stage. By the time of his farewell address to the Texas legislature in January 1969, things were not as they had once been. The House galleries were no longer packed when he spoke, and the only time his thirty-five-minute speech was interrupted with applause was when he mentioned the efforts of his wife, Nellie, to improve the grounds of the capitol.[25]

Texas Monthly editor Paul Burka characterized Connally as "the greatest Texas governor of the century" because he "saw the dark side of the Texas stereotype—a self-satisfaction, a narrowness, a confusion of size with greatness, and an obsession with myth that kept the State from realizing its full potential. What's more, he said so. He made Texans see that they weren't as good as they thought that they were."[26]

3

PRESTON SMITH

Spectacular feats are being performed in the game of Texas politics today. Never in Texas history have so few done so much to so many in the interests of so few.

JOHN HENRY FAULK

Preston Smith wore polka-dot ties and eyeglass frames with no lenses.

THE ODDS WERE against Preston Smith's ever becoming governor. He was from Lubbock, and no Texan had been elected governor who lived that far west. No Texan had made the jump from lieutenant governor to the Governor's Mansion since the Civil War—except by succession caused by a governor's death or impeachment. However, Smith felt that he was prepared to govern Texas, having served six years in the House, six years in the Senate, and six years as lieutenant governor. Although the popular Ben Barnes and John Connally disliked Smith, Smith defeated a large field of outstanding Texans for the post, including Connally's handpicked candidate, Eugene Locke, who came in fifth place in the primary.

John Connally was finishing his third term as governor, a term he had not particularly wanted to serve. When asked why Connally ran for the third term, Ben Barnes recalls: "He obviously didn't want Preston Smith to be governor. I think Connally was interested in holding the party together, and there wasn't anybody around to fill the leadership void."[1] Some, including Preston Smith and Roy Evans, the former president of the AFL-CIO, speculate that Connally could not have won reelection for a fourth term.[2]

Smith had governed Texas in Connally's absence for 277 days—including during Connally's five-week African safari. While Connally was on safari, Smith met with editorial boards and reporters around the state and reminded them that Connally had made a campaign issue of former governor Price Daniel's running for more than two terms. Connally had even mentioned in his first address to the legislature that gubernatorial terms should be limited to two. Smith then told members of the press that a man of Connally's integrity most certainly would not contradict his convictions by running for a fourth term. Smith charged that Connally's friends were trying to get him to violate his principles by persuading him to consider a fourth term. Smith found that each time that he predicted that Connally would not seek a fourth term, his own campaign received great press. Smith repeatedly quoted Connally's statements about the dangers inherent in serving multiple successive terms in office. He reminded voters that as recently as 1963, Connally had asked the legislature to recommend for voter approval a constitutional amendment that would limit a governor to two consecutive terms. In a press statement issued by his Austin office, Smith reasoned that even though many Texans might want Connally to run for a fourth term, they would thereby be pushing "the governor to violate his principles in this matter, and I would be very surprised to see Governor Connally violate his expressed principles to the people of Texas."[3]

Smith decided to run for governor; he informed Connally of this after the latter returned from Africa. Smith stated that although he didn't know Connally's plans, "I hoped that he would not be a candidate. I did not know whether I could defeat him. I thought I could. But whatever he did made no difference because my mind had been made up. I felt that the time had come for me to either run for governor then or not to run for governor."[4] Smith's boldness inured to his advantage while Connally took three full months to make his decision about whether to run for a fourth term. Others who were interested simply waited to see what Connally would do, whereas Smith campaigned and began getting secondary promises of support from those who otherwise would be supporting Connally.

Smith rightfully charged that no one else considering running for governor had the fortitude to do it without the incumbent's blessing. Smith recalled being certain that if he had not entered the race, Connally would have run for another term, even though Connally also probably believed that he could defeat Smith. According to Smith, "I'm sure that he knew that it would be a tough race. I was well-known throughout the State, and I do think that we could have made a good showing. Whether or not we could have defeated Governor Connally, no one will ever know."[5] Nevertheless, Smith believed that his decision to run caused Connally to choose not to do so.[6] In December, Connally announced that he would not run for reelection.

Eleven candidates filed to run for governor in the Democratic primary. In addition to Preston Smith, they included: a Uvalde rancher and banker, former state representative Dolph Briscoe; a Dallas radio operator, Gordon McLendon; a Dallas attorney, Eugene Locke; former attorney general Waggoner Carr; a Dallas insurance executive and son of a former governor, Pat O'Daniel; a Houston lawyer, former secretary of state John Hill; and a three-time unsuccessful gubernatorial candidate, Don Yarborough, among others. Most of the candidates had similar views on most issues; Yarborough was the lone liberal.

Smith had a running start and stood out from the crowd by constantly touting his experience. During 1968, he traveled the state—about 51,000 miles in a car—and sent 400,000 personalized letters asking for support, 47,000 of which were mailed to "Smith" households with the plea that it was time that someone with that name lived in the Governor's Mansion. Smith told Associated Press reporter Garth Jones that the Smith campaign had, through sheer effort, outpaced "all other twelve candidates combined. My greatest source of confidence in this race is the fact that I have had so many people involved on my behalf. We have more than 430 chairmen in cities and towns over the State. I have made about 1,200 speeches and visited 391 towns and cities."[7] Since no candidate won a majority of the votes in the primary, a runoff between Smith and Yarborough took place. The Texas Election Bureau reported the following tallies: Yarborough 422,423; Smith 382,335; Carr 257,202; Briscoe 225,610; Locke 218,712; Hill 155,076; and O'Daniel 47,167. Vote counts for the remaining candidates trailed considerably from there.[8] With the moderates and conservatives united behind a single candidate, Smith had an advantage over the liberal Yarborough. Smith won the runoff 756,909 to 620,726.

Republican hopes for taking the governor's office were high. Smith would face Paul Eggers, an oil-and-gas tax lawyer from Wichita Falls. The Republican consensus was that the Nixon campaign would run well in Texas and that the Humphrey ticket would run poorly, based in part on the riots at the 1968 Democratic National Convention in Chicago. But Smith's eighteen years of grassroots activism (compared to Eggers's nine months on the campaign trail) allowed him to reach his lifelong goal, and he beat Eggers by 400,000 votes, 1,659,478 to 1,252,952.

The governorship was set to pass from John Connally, the nationally admired sophisticated visionary, to an unpretentious movie-house operator who had grown up in a community called Corn Hill.

To highlight the difference the change in governor would make, one need only look at the inaugural-ball preparations. Lieutenant governor–elect Ben Barnes asked Robert Goulet to perform at the festivities, which Goulet agreed to do without charge. Barnes recalls that

One of Texas's 47,000 "Smiths" becomes governor, 1970.

after informing Preston Smith of this, the governor-elect made it clear that he had never heard of Robert Goulet, which surprised Barnes, since even though Goulet had by then been out of the limelight for a while, "he was one of the biggest stars on Broadway, in movies, and in the recording industry. In 1960, he'd originated the role of Lancelot in the first Broadway run of *Camelot,* starring with Richard Burton and Julie Andrews in the performance that first gained him national fame."[9] However, Smith indicated that he had not heard of the play. In his first veto since being elected governor, issued even before being sworn into office, Smith nixed the Goulet performance. Barnes called to rescind the invitation, and Glen Campbell and Jimmy Dean performed instead. The relationship between the newly elected governor and the newly elected lieutenant governor was off to a shaky start.

Unlike his predecessor, Smith failed in his inaugural address and his address to the Legislature to express a vision for things to come. Smith's inaugural address dealt vaguely with "fairness and justice," and he readily admitted that he would speak generally rather than specifically. He said to the legislature in his State of the State address: "The Connally Administration has been unquestionably one of great and generally productive activity in the field of long-range planning. I am sure that no other six years in our history have been so fruitful in that sense."[10] Smith's goals for his administration, by comparison, were modest. He called for the establishment of two new medical schools and a dental college. Beyond that, Smith put forth no concrete plans. He spoke of insurance concerns, prison matters, water planning, law enforcement, pollution control, constitutional revision, and other matters. However, he spoke with timid language, hedging things with phrases such as "it is my recommendation" or "I would be interested in" or "I would like to see." As a product of the legislature, he deferred to legislators' vision rather than seizing upon the opportunity to lead them. For example, his statement on pollution control, in its entirety, ran: "Whatever reasonable changes that, in the wisdom of the Legislature, are needed to strengthen our statutes on water and air pollution and the environment thereof will be favorably viewed by me. Attention should also be given to the growing problem of solid waste disposal."[11]

Smith understood the politics of getting things done and the procedures that could be used to stop things from happening. However, he had little vision for the future of Texas. As former *Dallas Times Herald* reporter Ernie Stromberger recounts, "Preston Smith was the product of the good old boys in the Senate," someone immersed in a system in which those in power consolidated their power "to help the people back home" rather than to pursue "any grand visions" the way Connally had.[12] Smith was an insider who relied on other insiders. That was why he appointed Bob Bullock and others who helped him use the power of the office to raise funds for a reelection campaign. Smith lacked Connally's connections to business; he also lacked Connally's focus on the big picture. Smith "was just sort of a caretaker type of governor who was just happy to be there and enjoy the perks of the office. He'd get into the state airplane and fly back to Lubbock every weekend, play bridge with his friends, and that was his idea of a good time."[13]

To be sure, Smith loved the job and relished enacting his role with the public, basking in having people see him as the governor. In spare moments, he would greet tourists in the capitol rotunda and would have breakfast each morning at the Driskill Hotel, where he would make himself available to the public at large. Longtime legislator Delwin Jones remembers that any Texan "could sit down, have breakfast with him, and visit with him at the Driskill. He was a great believer in that."[14]

Smith was similarly available to legislators. In contrast to the difficulty that legislators had had in meeting with Connally, Smith had an open-door policy with legislators. At times, he would answer his own phone. Smith kept a small staff of about thirty people in the capitol.

Being a creature of the legislature, Smith understood its workings better than many other governors, but he also misjudged it. He recommended a $320 million increase in state revenues, but did little to try to persuade legislators that the increase was necessary. When the legislature failed to pass the budget with Smith's proposed increase, he vetoed the no-tax budget and worked to pass it during a special session. Further embarrassment came with the appointment of Senator Dorsey Hardeman to the State Board of Insurance. As lieutenant governor, Smith had relied on the often tactless and overbearing Hardeman to deliver votes. To Smith's surprise, eleven of the thirty-one senators signed a pact to vote against Hardeman, denying him the two-thirds vote required for confirmation. Before this event, confirmation of all former members of the Senate had been virtually automatic: "Smith repeatedly reminded the eleven recalcitrant senators of such things as his veto power, but finally, as the session ended, admitted defeat by withdrawing Hardeman's appointment. The fiasco left lasting wounds."[15]

Later that year, Smith appointed his personal secretary's husband to a six-year term as the employers' representative on the Industrial Accident Board. Because Smith's appointee had spent most of his life working for state agencies and had never been an employer, his choice was controversial. The unions did not like the person Smith had selected, nor did the employers. In fact, Smith's appointee served in the $19,000-a-year job only until the appointment went before the Senate for confirmation, so Smith had to withdraw that nomination as well. This made the governor furious, and he determined that David Bell, the executive director of the Industrial Accident Board, was complicit in blocking the nomination and should be fired. Former aide Mike McKinney recalls using a light, diplomatic touch when approaching important people, such as agency directors or board members: "We'd identify ourselves and say, 'This is Mike McKinney. I'm in the governor's office. Governor Smith has been contacted by someone' or whatever the circumstances were, but we wouldn't say things like, 'The governor requests that you—' Instead, we would say things like, 'We'd appreciate any help.'"[16]

In this particular case, however, McKinney was forced to be considerably less accommodating and considerably more forceful. He recalls that he and his colleagues said, on the governor's orders, that they were there at Governor Smith's request. Then they delivered an ultimatum: terminate David Bell by the end of the day, or the governor would take the appropriation bill that was sitting on his desk and line-item-veto the executive director's salary and the salary of the two gubernatorial appointments they were then addressing.[17] McKinney recalls that the two political appointees whose jobs were thus threatened had been hired after their friends begged the governor to give them the jobs. In the end, "Governor Smith didn't follow through. But he did line-item-veto the salary of the executive director."[18]

Smith understood the power of the office and was not reluctant to use it. A vindictive Smith took delight in embarrassing people whom he knew had not voted for him. At the Dallas Press Club's Gridiron Dinner, he was asked by the club president's wife whether he planned to sign the bill that would create the University of Texas at Dallas. Smith replied by mentioning his failure to carry Dallas County in 1968, adding, "I plan to give it [the bill] the same consideration that the voters of Dallas gave me last year."[19] Accordingly, he vetoed the bill and demanded changes, effectively switching it from a four-year university to an upper-level institution offering only junior, senior, and graduate courses. These changes had to be made before he would sign a second version.

Because of Smith's background in the Senate and the habit of "bringing things home" to his district, he wanted a pharmacy school, and a medical school for the university in his hometown, Texas Technological College. In a bill to change the name of the institution to

Texas Tech University, Smith had caused to be inserted quietly into the legislation language that would require the appointment of nine new members of the board of regents, causing the terms of all current board members to expire. This allowed Smith, in his first year, to appoint the entire board of regents.

The regents at the University of Texas were endeavoring to build a great system with a series of new buildings, but the governor from Lubbock had different plans. He stipulated that he would not allow those vast building projects to proceed until after he had signed a bill for the medical school at Texas Tech or the pharmacy school at Texas Tech. He was skillful at linking his pet projects with the pet projects of others so that he would get his way. McKinney notes that he would say things such as, "'Well, look, I'm the governor. I have the ability to let these things go or to stop them because I can sign or veto a bill, or I can take care of a line-item veto.' He'd say, 'You know, you might get your UT–Dallas, you might get your upper divisions in Tyler, but, it won't be until after I get a pharmacy school' at Texas Tech University. And they know it all funnels to that one place."[20]

What McKinney refers to as the "old-boy network," Ernie Stromberger refers to as "pork-barrel politics." Both agree that Smith knew how to wheel and deal to get what he wanted, even though his methods went against Connally's. Stromberger says that Smith was good at pork-barrel politics, the very "system that Connally had tried to derail when he created the Higher Education Coordinating Board because members of the Senate were setting up all of these colleges in their hometowns because it created jobs, and it brought wealth to the community. It was 'bringing home the bacon.' Smith was good at that because that's the world he grew up in."[21]

Given the lack of opponents in the Democratic primary, and the Republican Party's poor results in the previous election, Smith was assured another two-year term as governor. After winning reelection, he gave legislators, as he had done two years earlier, a synopsis of matters of state as he saw them, with recommendations. His program required neither "drastic reductions in the budget nor drastic new tax programs."[22]

However, despite Smith's ease at winning reelection, there was a cloud over the capitol. It had to do with a couple of bills passed in 1969 and allegations that Smith and Speaker of the House Gus Mutscher might have taken bribes to get them passed. The day of the inauguration, the Securities and Exchange Commission filed civil suits alleging that certain legislators had advanced legislation in return for money. In short, Sharpstown State Bank of Houston gave loans to legislators, who in turn bought stock in National Bankers Life Insurance Company. These officeholders were able to sell their shares only weeks later for a nice profit—Smith made $62,500—owing to the insider manipulations of Frank Sharp. Sharp owned both Sharpstown State Bank and National Bankers Life Insurance Company. Sharp arranged the stock and loan deals in exchange for legislators' commitments to pass two banking bills that benefited his businesses. Both the House and Senate quickly passed the bills that he had promoted. While Smith and Mutscher admitted taking the loans and the stock profits, they denied that there was any connection between those financial transactions and the subsequent passage of the bills.

Smith did two things relating to this scandal, one indefensible and another that inadvertently proved to be his redemption. He allowed a special legislative session to consider Sharp's banking bills. Fortunately for Smith, however, once the controversial bills had passed, he vetoed them. He had been advised to do so by former governor Allan Shivers. While the Democratic Party, the legislature, and the lives of many of his associates were being torn apart by the scandal and the associated ongoing investigation, Smith appeared to be unaffected. In a speech at the Headliners Club in February 1971, Smith said: "I'd like to quote from the book of John—not John Connally. Let he who is without stock throw the first rock!"[23]

Ernie Stromberger describes Smith as having an inner toughness, something proved by how he survived the Sharpstown scandal: "He skated through the whole thing like a stone wall. That was kind of characteristic of the people he grew up with in the Senate. They had the guts to just run over people and just shrug it off. To him, the people he was close to operated this way."[24]

By 1972, Speaker Mutscher and others had been convicted on bribery charges, and in the fall elections, over half of the House of Representatives were freshmen, compared with an average turnover rate of 20 percent. It was a new day in Texas politics. Outwardly, Smith behaved as if nothing unusual had occurred, even though all three of the state's top Democratic officials—Smith himself, Mutscher, and Barnes—had been forced out of office by fallout from the investigation.

The last several days that Smith was in office were hectic. He strove to appoint candidates whom he favored to as many positions as he could in the time remaining. Smith aide Mike McKinney recalls that during those last few days, they worked throughout the weekend. They appointed some people to positions without finding out whether they would be willing to serve. McKinney notes, "I don't remember whether the secretary of state's office was open to take the appointment letters, but I know that we took a lot of appointment documents over to the secretary of state's office on Monday before the Tuesday inauguration."[25]

However, despite the last-minute push, there was simply not enough time left before Governor Smith's term ended at noon on inauguration day. On that Tuesday, most offices were shut down, and most staff members were already gone. McKinney recalls, "I picked Smith up at the mansion and drove him over to the capitol. He and Mrs. Smith attended the ceremony, and then we went straight to the airport. I put him on the state plane. We didn't ask Briscoe if we could use it—we just made it on, and the pilots took him back to Lubbock. The phone in the governor's office stopped ringing right before Christmas because everybody kind of figured out that that was it."[26]

DOLPH BRISCOE

The Chicken Ranch was America's oldest continuously operating whorehouse. It was run by a madam named Edna Milton, who used an iron hand to make sure the big old white house in the woods near La Grange was as good a house as a house could be good. It can be argued that everyone knew it was there. It can be argued that countless young men who grew up to be leaders of Texas visited the place. It can be argued that Sheriff Jim Flournoy was negligent in not closing it. But the Chicken Ranch was an institution of sorts, beyond the law.

In the summer of '73, a Houston television news reporter, Marvin Zindler, began to report on the whorehouse and asked the governor and the attorney general why they did not close the place. Gov. Dolph Briscoe reacted with great indignity upon learning from Zindler that Texas actually had a whorehouse in it, and if he had to, he would have the Rangers close it—after all, they had done everything else.

The pressure built, and on August 2, 1973, Sheriff Jim closed the house. He later said, "It's been there all my life and all my daddy's life and never caused anybody any trouble. Every large city in Texas has things one thousand times worse."

RON STONE, "August 2, 1973," *Book of Texas Days*

Governor Dolph Briscoe and First Lady Janie Briscoe, 1974.

WHEN DOLPH BRISCOE was elected governor of Texas, critics pointed out that he owned more land in Texas than any other Texan, ranching over one million acres, and that he held more bank stock than any other Texan. His supporters countered that he had more to lose if things went wrong, so he was perfectly suited for the job. Briscoe grew up in Uvalde as the son of a twice-broke rancher who formed a ranching partnership with Governor Ross Sterling the year Dolph was born. By the time he reached adulthood, Dolph Briscoe was a wealthy, politically informed young man, having had as a mentor and friend John Nance Garner, the former vice president and a fellow citizen of Uvalde. In fact, at the conclusion of his tenure as governor, Dolph Briscoe stated that his governorship had been guided by the philosophy of his mentor, "my old friend from Uvalde, the late Vice-President John Nance Garner, who said, 'Government should do only two things: safeguard the lives and property of our people and ensure that each of us has a chance to work out his destiny according to his talents.'"[1]

Briscoe's main talents were ranching and banking. His ranches covered more territory than some countries. It was at his Catarina Ranch that John Connally had planned his run for governor some years earlier with key advisors from across Texas. Briscoe would begin his campaign for governor in the same way, from the same place. He invited key people from all parts of Texas to the ranch to solicit their support; to hunt; to eat dishes of peppers, chili, and skillet biscuits with barbeque; and to stay in his house, which could comfortably sleep over one hundred people. When asked why he would consider running for governor, Briscoe said:

It sounds corny, I know, to say that I'm concerned over the future of this state. But that's true. I wonder sometimes why I would get mixed up in something like a governor's race instead of just coming out here and hunting or fishing. Winston Churchill summed it up pretty well by saying that he wanted to do everything worthwhile that he could while he was here on this earth. I think you should try to serve wherever you can. I would like to be able to contribute something to the growth and prosperity of this state and also the stability of this state.[2]

It is often said that timing is a big part of political success. It is also said that whom God wishes to destroy, he first gives political power. Both of these factors played favorably into Briscoe's hands. Briscoe, a man of unquestioned integrity, was viewed as a political outsider, even though he had served years before as a state representative. He would run for governor on the heels of the biggest political scandal that Texas had ever endured: Sharpstown. This scandal would take down Governor Preston Smith, Speaker Gus Mutscher, and, incredibly, the rising star of the Democratic Party, Lieutenant Governor Ben Barnes. Briscoe's campaign called for a fresh start in Austin.

Although it was not known at the time—and this occurred completely without Briscoe's knowledge or consent—Briscoe would get campaign help from an unlikely source: the Nixon White House. The agenda in Washington was to cripple the Democratic establishment in Texas and, specifically, to remove the popular Ben Barnes—whom Lyndon Johnson had dramatically touted as a future president from Texas—from elective office.

In November 1969, despite having been led by Democratic governors for decades, Virginia and New Jersey elected Republican governors. In both states, a significant split, similar to that in Texas, existed between the conservative and liberal branches of the Democratic Party—and in both states, President Nixon was popular. The prize, however, would be the strongest Democratic voting bloc in the South: Texas. In a meeting with U.S. attorney general John Mitchell in the offices of the Committee to Re-elect the President (CREEP), Senator John Tower and his state campaign-finance chairman, Julian Zimmerman, expressed concern about the career of Ben Barnes and his possible challenge to Tower. Zimmerman recounts that Mitchell dismissed the concern, saying, "Don't worry about Ben Barnes. There's an investigation going on that will remove him from the political picture."[3]

The day before the gubernatorial inauguration in 1971, rumors circulated at a victory dinner. Three thousand Democrats had gathered to eat steak and listen to Wayne Newton sing. Despite the official cel-

ebration, the mood dimmed as rumors spread throughout the audito-
rium that the Securities and Exchange Commission (SEC) had filed a
lawsuit that day, and indictments of significant Democratic politicians
were expected to follow soon. With curious timing—which would
ensure inauguration-day headlines—newspapers confirmed that the
SEC had filed a civil suit against some legislators for allegedly taking
bribes. And in the following weeks and months, the Sharpstown scandal unfolded like a slow-motion catastrophe.

Although no credible evidence linked Barnes to the scheme, it
is clear that he was the target of the Nixon administration's political
maneuvering. The Justice Department granted Frank Sharp full im-
munity in exchange for guilty pleas on two felony charges and his full
cooperation and testimony. In agreeing to the deal, Sharp received a
mere three years' probation and a five-thousand-dollar fine. In Babe
Schwartz's analysis: "Frank Sharp was whoring for the feds and for
Nixon and Connally. And Barnes wouldn't say anything unkind about
Connally if he died first, but, hell, Connally was a part of the Nixon
administration, and Connally was as much responsible for trying to
destroy the Democratic Party in Texas as Nixon was."[4]

Although Barnes was not a target of the investigation, Justice Department leaks, investigations, and rumors were designed to implicate
him. In addition, the Internal Revenue Service ordered audits of many
Democratic officials and candidates. The politicians saw this as more
than mere coincidence. As former lieutenant governor Hobby recalls,
"When I ran for lieutenant governor in 1972, my runoff opponent
was John Connally's brother Wayne. John Connally was secretary of
the treasury at that time, and he opened an income-tax investigation
on me."[5]

In a taped White House conversation on September 4, 1971, President Nixon and Attorney General Mitchell discussed a delicate problem concerning Will Wilson, one of Nixon's assistant attorneys general, whom many believe was the force behind the investigation. As a
Texas Democrat, Wilson had run for, and lost, Lyndon Johnson's Senate seat in 1961 and competed in the Democratic primary for governor
against John Connally in 1962. After those defeats, Wilson left the
Democratic Party in great bitterness. Ironically, Wilson had been an

associate of Frank Sharp in the 1960s. This association was a cause of concern for Mitchell:

> MITCHELL: You have a prime and vital interest in the politics in Texas. This Sharp thing has just about destroyed the Democrat party down there. Uh, Wilson—
> NIXON: The governor is involved—Wilson with Sharp—
> MITCHELL: The governor, the speaker of the House, the head of the Democratic party, et cetera, et cetera. So, we have a hard choice to make as to whether to admit that Wilson, as a lawyer for Sharp, was involved with the Sharp situation—which of course he was, in some areas. Not illegally—there's never been anything illegal done. Or we could toss him to the wolves and get him out of here and say he's just part of that Texas so-and-so, and then we're losing the stroke that we have in Texas with the leg up on the Democrats. So, it's a choice that is, uh, rather difficult, and of course I've been quite close to this picture, and I thought it was something I ought to run by you.[6]

Richard Nixon's first reaction was to find out what John Connally had to say on the subject:

> NIXON: Did Connally talk to you about it?
> MITCHELL: Connally and I have talked about this situation, particularly in trying to take care of his boy Ben Barnes—
> NIXON: He's in it too?
> MITCHELL: Yeah.
> NIXON: Damn right.
> MITCHELL: He is not involved in the fixing of the legislation, like the other Democrats are, but he's got a lot of things to answer to.[7]

The investigations, rumors, and leaks initiated in Washington did indeed give Barnes much to answer for. The voters were angry at corruption in the capitol, and any incumbent politician therefore had some explaining to do. Less than two months before the primary election, a jury convicted Speaker of the House Gus Mutscher and two others for their involvement in the Sharpstown affair. Their sentence would be five years' probation.

Barnes and others would be found guilty by association. In a four-person race for governor, the former rising star of the party would come in third. Governor Preston Smith would finish a distant fourth. Dolph Briscoe was in a good place at a good time. In the Democratic runoff, Briscoe would be the clean, conservative candidate facing liberal State Representative Sissy Farenthold—whom he would handily defeat. He would go on to beat his Republican opponent, Henry Grover, by approximately 100,000 votes.

On May 9, 1972, in a taped, Oval Office conversation with John Connally days after the Texas Democratic primary election, President Nixon pretended that he did not know the outcome of the Texas elections, perhaps to get Connally to provide more background information on the political climate in Texas. Connally said to Nixon, "You have in this country unrest of enormous proportion. It's true all over, certainly in Texas, aggravated in Texas by the scandals, to the point where the incumbent governor [Preston Smith] got eight percent of

Microphone problems, 1975.

the votes, and my good friend Ben Barnes got about eighteen percent. And a woman [Sissy Farenthold] beat the hell out of him, and Dolph Briscoe—Barnes couldn't even get in the runoff."[8]

Nixon again indicated a lack of up-to-date knowledge of the Texas politics, leading Connally to explain it to him in more detail. Nixon asked Connally about the results of the Democratic primary.

> CONNALLY: Oh! Just murder! They just wiped everybody out—
> they beat him—they've got a runoff between Dolph Briscoe
> and this woman Sissy Farenthold, who's a big McGovernite,
> who's for—oh, hell, Ben Barnes got eighteen percent of the
> vote!
> NIXON: Who, who in the hell is Briscoe?
> CONNALLY: Dolph Briscoe is a friend of mine, he's a farmer and
> rancher who's a product of this guy Walker, from Memphis,
> Tennessee. He's a boy that this PR firm just took. And he
> never made a damn speech, wouldn't keep his appointments.
> Ain't nothing wrong with him, but he was just nothing. Just
> a pure media campaign, and the scandals in Texas just wiped
> the slate.[9]

Nixon continued to elicit more information from Connally:

> NIXON: Gosh, I didn't know.
> CONNALLY: Oh, they wiped 'em out. Just unbelievable. Every-
> body's stunned.
> NIXON: I can't understand Barnes getting beat—He's a very at-
> tractive fellow—
> CONNALLY: Oh, it's unbelievable! One of the really bright young
> men. And was no way connected with the scandals! But they
> thought he was. And, hell, this woman—this Sissy Farenthold,
> who's for legalized abortion, who's for legalized marijuana, a
> very radical woman! Beat the hell out of him! Got—beat him
> by 150,000 votes![10]

Years later, both Bob Haldeman, Nixon's chief of staff, and John Mitchell, Nixon's attorney general, would apologize to Ben Barnes for their role in targeting his political career. Dolph Briscoe was the un-witting beneficiary of their connivances. Mark White recalls that his mentor, Dolph Briscoe, entered office on the moral high ground in the wake of the Sharpstown scandal. That scandal had dashed the political ambitions of many others, incumbents and hopefuls, even those, such as Ben Barnes, who were not involved in the scandal, "but just happened to be in the capitol when it happened and got swept out. Otherwise, I think Barnes would have been elected. He came in a pretty distant third. It's kind of a lesson that when things start to fall apart in politics, they can fall apart very fast. Barnes was thought to be the favorite up to the last three or four weeks."[11]

The electorate seemed ready for a leader with unquestioned integrity. Mark White refers to Dolph Briscoe as "the finest, most decent man, I know. He is just an incredibly good guy. I never heard him say a word in private in the governor's office that he couldn't have said on the steps of First Baptist Church."[12]

When asked about the essential qualities of a good governor, Lieutenant Governor Hobby said, "Well, first of all, he has to be a good person. Of the governors that I served with, I say that Dolph Briscoe was the best person—most humane—most understanding—and most compassionate."[13] Nonetheless, Briscoe's chief primary opponent, Sissy Farenthold, often referred to him as a "bowl of pabulum." However, after the noisy scandal in the capitol, the quiet of the Briscoe administration seemed to many to be a welcome respite.

Commentators regularly describe Dolph Briscoe as a "caretaker governor." Tax revenues from the booming 1970s allowed him to make good on his "no new taxes" campaign pledge and to preside over a sound fiscal period. Briscoe expected little of government and, consequently, did not feel compelled to be an activist governor. In fact, he spent much of his administration at his ranch in Uvalde.

In his first address to the legislature, Briscoe dubbed the theme of his administration "cooperation for progress." He pledged access for legislators and called for an end to political rivalries, which lead to stalemates, confusion, and inefficiency. Briscoe said that his top priority would be the development of a "strong, clear code of ethics." He told the legislators that ethics legislation "must be a tough and definitive statement of the demand by the people that there be a return of morality in state government. It must be specific and clear in stating these requirements so that there can be no question of whether, in a given instance, the rule had been violated."[14] In addition, Briscoe called for a "no tax" budget, a streamlined penal code, the reinstatement of the death penalty in certain cases, and tougher property-protection laws. In each of these areas, he prevailed. As he told legislators in his address, "the most persistent lobbyist you will see this session is the governor of Texas."[15] Briscoe had less success with his education and environmental initiatives. As *Dallas Times Herald* reporter Dave Montgomery notes, "Dolph Briscoe has completed his first crucial test as the State's chief executive, proving perhaps that he is neither a bowl of pabulum, nor a block of granite."[16]

However, the "pabulum" image persisted, with critics charging that the government was not being led by Briscoe, but by his wife, Janie. It became a running joke in the capitol to refer to "Governor and Mr. Briscoe." Indeed, the governor's wife seemed omnipresent. It was her habit to stand at his side at press conferences, often interrupting him, and seldom did anyone meet with the governor without Mrs. Briscoe being present. Mrs. Briscoe responded to charges that she was running the government, saying, "I'm not the governor, and I don't want anybody to think otherwise. Maybe all this has come about because Dolph and I have a good friendship, as well as a good marriage, but I have no official capacity, and I do no work at all that is political. I want to be governor about as much as I want to be the first ape on the moon."[17] While trying to help the introverted Briscoe, the extroverted first lady, who tended to scold reporters for being too pushy and who frequently interrupted press conferences to give her husband time to reflect upon answers to reporters' questions, made him appear weak. As columnist Bill Porterfield put it, "Dolph Briscoe's governorship will count for little in time. He never disturbed the eagles of finance who have ruled Texas for so long. Even if he had been a strutting cock, like Shivers or Connally, he would not have. They are all birds of a feather, sitting on a high perch in the hen house. The difference is that Shivers and Connally were real roosters. Briscoe was henpecked."[18]

Governor Briscoe also faced criticism for his work habits. He once went sixty-one days without holding a press conference, and in 1975, reporters used state aircraft flight logs to determine that Briscoe spent ninety days in Uvalde in the first ten months of the year, including thirty-nine workdays. Lee Jones, reporting for the *Dallas Times Herald*, cited an example of Briscoe's "government in absentia" style: "Forrest Smith, whom Briscoe replaced last month as chairman of the Texas Youth Council, tried for more than a year to speak with Briscoe about the problems of troubled youth in Texas. But all such efforts failed. A letter written to the governor requesting a meeting of great urgency has not been answered."[19] Legislators threatened to turn in a request that the Department of Public Safety search the state for the missing governor. His characteristic low profile contributed to a perception of gubernatorial weakness. Frank Erwin, a political powerhouse and former chairman of the board of regents at the University of Texas, was a vocal critic of the governor: "It doesn't matter if you have a governor or not because he's gone about four-fifths of the time. He's furnished no leadership of any kind."[20]

Despite these problems, Briscoe was in an enviable political position. He continued to be viewed as a reprieve from the brash and self-serving politicians of the Sharpstown period. The party was unified, and the economy was the beneficiary of strong oil and gas tax revenues. Briscoe announced his bid for reelection at a fund-raising dinner—the largest in state history—after jockeying to avoid answering reporters' questions about his intentions for a couple of months. Dave Montgomery of the *Dallas Times Herald* sized Briscoe up as follows: "Although colorless and sometimes personally inaccessible—at least to the press—Briscoe projects the image of a down-to-earth hardworker, a man intent on simply being an honest public servant. He has done nothing to violate the public trust, and in the age of Sharpstown and Watergate, that is the most essential prerequisite for a public official."[21] He sailed into his second term, beating Republican Jim Granberry by a two-to-one margin.

While the four previous administrations had all increased state taxes—even though revenues from existing taxes had continued to increase anyway—Briscoe made good on his vow that under his watch the Texas government would live within its income without any new taxes. Moreover, during his six years in office—the Constitution was amended in 1974 to change the length of the governor's term from two years to four years—state aid for public schools increased by $1.2 billion. This compared with an $835 million total increase in the four previous administrations. In addition, Briscoe recommended that the legislature eliminate the 4 percent sales tax on gas and electricity bills, saving consumers approximately $250 million per year. However, Briscoe was most proud of his increased funding initiatives for the Highway Department. Ever a fiscal conservative, Briscoe reduced the staff of the governor's office over a period of time through attrition and transfers.

In his first address to the legislature, Briscoe called for a constitutional convention to rewrite the state constitution of 1876: "This administration and this legislature will be remembered, perhaps above all administrations and legislatures of this century, for constitutional revision."[22] However, after a contentious convention, in which objectionable proposals, such as annual legislative sessions, were added, Briscoe changed his mind. He asked voters to reject all new constitutional amendments that would have led to the adoption of the new constitution. With Briscoe's urging, voters in 250 out of 254 counties voted against its adoption.

Despite his gubernatorial successes, Briscoe was defeated for re-election in the Democratic primary by Attorney General John Hill. Comptroller Bob Bullock, in his own inimitable way, said that "Texas voters have a choice between a proven governor and a 'son of a bitch'"—referring in the latter case to Hill.[23] With the majority of Democratic primary voters ready for a change, they went with the "son of a bitch." Briscoe, whom voters perceived as a "do nothing" governor, was now free to return to his beloved Catarina Ranch in Uvalde.

5

WILLIAM P. CLEMENTS

I ain't being critical when I say that I used to be ignernt myself about Republikins. I was plumb growed 'fore I ever seen one! Never will forgit. I was sitting out on the back porch reading the Dallas Morning News. *I seen a picture in the paper and it said, "Thomas E. Dewey." Then next to that was the word "Republican."*

Well, the truth come to me in a blinding flash, and I called Mama.

I said, "Mama, come here quick. Did you ever see a Republikin?"

She said, "No, I ain't."

I said, "Wish you'd look at that!"

She stares at the picture and says, "Lord have mercy! Is that one?"

I says, "Shore is!"

She says, "Why hit's got clothes on, ain't it!"

There you are. Me and Mama was both Republikin ignernt. Just like you folks and everybody else in Texas.

You know why?

'Cause we've gone and left open season on Republikins in Texas for so long, we done thinned 'em out to nothing.

JOHN HENRY FAULK, *The Uncensored John Henry Faulk*

In 1983, Bill and Rita Clements became the first Republicans since Reconstruction to reside in the Governor's Mansion.

IT HAS BEEN said that the need to be liked is a wonderful characteristic in a spaniel, but not in a leader. If Bill Clements ever felt a need to be liked, he disguised it. Never one to pander or play to an audience, Governor Clements called things as he saw them. He has been described as blunt, open, cranky, direct, and to the point. These traits were viewed as either refreshingly businesslike or mean-spirited. Former Clements staffer Jim Francis explains, "Clements is the most immune politician I know about what people think. I don't think he gave two tinkers' damn for one millisecond what people thought."[1] Few could think that such a character could be elected governor—particularly as a Republican.

One experienced observer of the political scene in Texas, Paul Burka, thought that Clements's candidacy was virtually ignored, like those of other Republican gubernatorial candidates, because their defeat was seen as inevitable: "Clements disrupted this ritual, first by spending an astonishing amount of money and then by managing to project his blunt, cranky personality to an electorate that had not yet begun to grasp the full extent of its impatience with wavering, apologetic statesmen like Jimmy Carter. On television, Clements came across as unsophisticated and abrasive, but the Democrats who misread these traits as stupidity were not quite plugged in."[2]

Clements's down-home style played to the voters much better than the Democratic elite realized at first; similarly, they failed to realize how poorly their own candidate came across: "John Hill, Clements' opponent, was quiet and sophisticated. He spoke with a courtly lisp. Deep in some primitive lobe of the voters' brains, there was no contest. Nobody really wanted a gentleman as governor of Texas when it was possible to have a roughneck. On Election Day, the world as Texas had known it for a hundred years ended. All of a sudden, here was Bill Clements, a Republican, literally governing in his shirtsleeves."[3]

Clements grew up in Dallas and attended the University of Texas, where he met John Connally, and Southern Methodist University (SMU) before going to work as a roughneck in the oilfields of Texas. Recalls Clements, "Oil was a fascinating business; it represented a challenge—a romance if you will—that other businesses just didn't have for young people at that time. It was a frontier, glamorous, and a way to get rich quickly—at least in many people's minds."[4]

Clements's instincts were good. By the time he was thirty, he had founded a small drilling company made up largely of debt, two rigs, and two partners—the Southeastern Drilling Company. Within eight years, Clements bought out both partners and built the company into a large land and offshore company with twenty-nine drilling rigs. Three years later, the company landed the largest drilling contract ever awarded anywhere, to drill one thousand wells for the government-owned Argentine oil company, YPF. Clements, the businessman, was spending his time negotiating drilling contracts in India, Pakistan, Iran, Canada, and the United States.

Soon after, at the age of forty-seven, Clements first became politically involved after being asked to run for the United States Senate by the chairman of the Republican Party of Texas, Peter O'Donnell. Instead, Clements recruited George H. W. Bush to run, but promised to serve as Bush's finance chairman. Bush lost, but the political bug had planted its teeth firmly in Clements's flesh. In 1972, Clements would go on to raise money for Texans for Richard Nixon and would become cochairman of the Texas Committee to Re-elect the President. Clements set up offices all over the state. He was anything but a chair in name only. It was during this campaign that he met Rita Bass. Within three years, he would be divorced from his wife of thirty-five years, who did not share his interest in politics, and would be married to Rita Bass Clements.

Texans voted for Nixon over McGovern by a two-to-one margin. President Nixon nominated Bill Clements to serve as deputy secretary of defense. Secretary of the Treasury John Connally had pushed for the appointment: "Nixon had talked about the appointment with Connally, and Connally had assured him that Clements wanted the deputy's job rather than the job of secretary. Clements would be the chief operating officer of the Pentagon, which Nixon considered the sixth most important job in Washington, behind the president, vice-president, and the secretaries of State, Treasury, and Defense."[5] As the number two person at the Pentagon, Clements would manage the Department of Defense, administering a bureaucracy with three million employees and an eighty-billion-dollar budget.

Bill Clements's favorite verse in the Bible is in the third chapter of Ecclesiastes: "To everything there is a season and a time to every purpose under heaven." It was now Bill Clements's time to serve. He would be the first deputy secretary to serve the full four-year term. He concluded his tenure under Secretary of Defense Donald Rumsfeld, who had been a colleague of Gerald Ford's in the House of Representatives. Rumsfeld, who wanted his own team, got the president to offer a series of different cabinet posts to Clements. Clements stayed put, which did little to foster a good relationship between him and Rumsfeld.

In November 1977, Clements decided to run for governor. An overnight guest in the Clements home, former astronaut and U.S. senator Harrison "Jack" Schmitt (New Mexico), suggested that Clements run. Rita advised him to run, and she was his top advisor, having been active in grassroots Republican politics for years. After observing her husband on the stump, she wrote a list of constructive criticisms, which included admonitions to smile more, be more personal, be less gruff, learn state issues, shorten speeches, quit talking down to people, stop frowning, and stop saying "Let me finish!"[6] Nevertheless, there was to be no changing Bill Clements. He said that he would not change his hairstyle or how he dressed to change his public image. As he put it, such attempts at manipulating public perception are "sheer dishonesty. When I first started campaigning, these professional people came in. They were telling me there's a school in New York City, this so-called charm school, where they teach you how to dress, how to move your hands, how to speak. Baloney. Under no circumstances do I want to be anything but me."[7]

In the primary, he ran against Ray Hutchison, who was chair of the Texas Republican Party and a bond attorney from Dallas (and husband of current U.S. senator Kay Bailey Hutchison). Hutchison had tried to get Clements to commit to running for governor, but Clements said that he would not run. Once Hutchison was in the race, Clements announced that, in fact, he would be a candidate. Clements outspent Hutchison ten-to-one and defeated him by a three-to-one margin. In the Democratic primary, Attorney General John Hill defeated Governor Dolph Briscoe, the incumbent, handily. Preston Smith, the former governor, got less than 6 percent of the vote. Political strategist

On the campaign trail, Rita Clements admonished her husband not to bark,
"Let me finish!" to reporters.

Jim Francis calls this turn of events a perfect storm: "We were working hard at building a coalition that could get us elected. Then Hill
beat Briscoe, and that really helped us because you can say there's not
much difference between a Republican candidate and Dolph Briscoe.
But there was a big perceived difference between John Hill and a Republican. So it gave us a shot in the arm."[8]

   Hill anticipated an easy fall campaign, and Clements shifted into
overdrive, enlisting Briscoe supporters and describing the campaign
as one between an experienced businessman and a "liberal lawyer."
Hill made little effort to mend fences with Briscoe Democrats, while
one of Clements's first campaign stops included a reception at the
bank owned by Dolph Briscoe in Uvalde. Briscoe's children openly
supported the Clements effort. The campaign devised a rural strategy,
even though Republicans controlled only one courthouse in Texas:
Midland. Soon, the Clements campaign would have chairs in 244 of

the state's 254 counties. Gerald Ford and Ronald Reagan put personal differences aside to host fundraisers in Dallas and Houston. These fundraisers brought $1.2 million to the campaign's coffers.

Clements ran the campaign like a CEO. He hired the best in the industry for media, direct mail, and phone banking. John Connally cut endorsement commercials, saying that Texas needed a strong governor to stand up to the federal government. Clements was one of the first to realize the powerful political instincts of the young strategist Karl Rove.[9] Recalls Mike Toomey, "Clements was a good judge of people. When anyone came into the office, he would be listening and sizing them up like any good CEO would do. I think that he knew Karl Rove was brilliant and knew what he needed to do. Karl did have a proper map, and they hit it off. Clements trusted Rove."[10]

In the final month of the campaign, an unexpected bombshell burst, advancing the Clements efforts. Janie Briscoe, the former first lady, told the press that she believed that Bill Clements was better suited to be governor than John Hill was. Recalls Jim Francis, "It was a stunning revelation. We had been closing the gap on Hill, and we had our problems with Clements as a candidate, but we were making progress. However, when Janie Briscoe did that, it changed the dynamics of the election. It was still an unbelievable squeaker. Had she not done that, I'm not sure whether we would have won."[11]

Just more than two weeks before the election, a *Texas Monthly* poll showed Hill having an eleven-point lead, but 21 percent of the electorate was still undecided. Hill confidently asserted, "There is no way I will lose. We have enough votes to win, regardless of the turnout. The polls show I'm going straight up." Clements, meanwhile, claimed that his own poll showed that he and Hill were in a "dead heat."[12] In the end, Clements officially won the race by a margin of 16,909 votes out of 2.2 million votes cast. He promised to be an active governor. On the heels of the passive Briscoe administration, many saw benefit in such a change.

In his address to the Sixty-sixth Legislature, Clements stressed government accountability and fiscal responsibility. He called for a four-pronged "Taxpayer Bill of Rights," which would require a two-thirds vote of the legislature to pass any tax measure, give Texans the right to vote on initiatives and referenda, ban all personal and corporate income taxes, and give local voters the ability to call an election to ratify or reject taxes adopted by local governmental units. In addition, he called on the legislature to limit the terms of the governor, lieutenant governor, and attorney general to two four-year terms. His program was relatively small and largely unsuccessful. The Taxpayer Bill of Rights went nowhere. Few felt that his campaign rhetoric of returning a billion dollars to the taxpayers and cutting 25,000 governmental jobs would gain much legislative traction. Representative Pete Laney recalls Clements's attitude in his first term: "'This is the way we're going to run the business, and I'm the chief executive officer, and y'all can take it or leave it!' So the first bill he vetoed, we overrode to show him. He probably didn't take it too well because he didn't change a whole lot."[13]

This was the first override of a gubernatorial veto in thirty-eight years. There has not been another one since. While the Democratic majority organized itself to teach the autocratic governor his place, Republicans, led by Representative Lee Jackson of Dallas, joined forces to override the veto in order to prevent it looking like a party-line vote that would embarrass the Republicans. Clements called the legislators "a bunch of idiots."[14] Nonetheless, he told the press: "I got the message. Apparently, that comes under some kind of privilege they have. But I think that it's a very bad law."[15]

Corporate protocols differ markedly from the give-and-take negotiations that legislative progress requires. Laney recounts: "It took a while for Clements to understand that there were people who would help him with his program, but, that it was *his* program and that we weren't going to do all of his work for him. He came in to lecture us on how the bill was going to change, or he'd veto it. I told him, 'Governor, I was carrying this bill for you, but if you really think I care if it passes—you're wrong.' I walked out. In two minutes, he had me back in there and was saying, 'Let's work this out.'"[16]

In the campaign, Clements had vowed to get rid of "parasitic bureaucrats" and to trim state employment by 25,000 workers. To be sure, his relations with state workers were not good. As Sam Kinch put it: "Governor Bill Clements gave State bureaucrats a lecture Tuesday, but half of them didn't show up, and none of them responded to what the governor said. After a half-hour presentation, Clements said that he was ready for questions and/or comments. Nobody asked or said anything."[17] Clements asked a second and a third time for comments or questions, with a similar lack of response. He then arranged for meetings in their departments, but when only half of the 700 invited state workers showed up at the governor's request, Clements confessed that he did not know how to interpret the absence of the other half.

Times were good, and the treasury showed a surplus of $2.8 billion. However, Clements and Lieutenant Governor Hobby had differing spending priorities. Indeed, they had differing views of the role of government. Clements saw Hobby as a careless liberal, and Hobby grew increasingly exasperated by much of what Clements did. An example Hobby relates is representative of his exasperation:

> It was the custom on Tuesday mornings before the session for the governor, the lieutenant governor, and the Speaker to have breakfast at the Mansion. Everybody had things they wanted to bring up. Clements, one day, had something to do with prisons. I was tired of throwing water on the nutty ideas that Clements would bring back from his friends at the Dallas Country Club, so I suggested, "Governor, every Monday night, I meet with committee chairmen. Why don't you come to that meeting next Monday and present your ideas? If you can sell this to the nine guys—we will get it passed; if you can't—we won't." Pretty simple.[18]

Hobby notes that he bowed out and let the governor carry out his attempt to win over this particular audience on his own, with the results that Hobby no doubt had predicted, but that took the governor by surprise and left him permanently embittered: "He did—and I did not—attend. I was going to let Governor Clements talk. The two senators who were most interested in corrections were Ray Farabee and Grant Jones, and apparently, they just jumped on him and discounted his unworthy ideas. He never came back on the Senate side for the rest of that session."[19]

As head of the Legislative Budget Board, Hobby proposed an increase in spending of 22 percent over the previous state budget. Clements, on the other hand, wanted to return one billion dollars to the taxpayers and thought that this sum could be found by spending less on public education and by reducing a proposed teacher pay raise. Hobby criticized the governor's plan, while Clements called Hobby's wishes a "letter to Santa Claus."[20] Clements was unable to get his billion dollars of tax relief, and he failed to pass his Taxpayer Bill of Rights legislation. In addition, the initiative and referendum concept he was pushing had been doomed from the start. He gave the Legislature an F and told Sam Attlesey of the *Dallas Morning News,* "This is my first legislative session, and I wouldn't recommend it to anybody."[21]

However, as a fiscal conservative, Clements had successes. He had advocated reducing the number of state employees by 25,000, which amounted to 15 percent of the full-time equivalents in 1980. The legislature agreed to a 5 percent reduction in state employment per year. Further, by wielding the line-item veto, the governor was able to cut $252 million from the budget with a stroke of his pen. However, $30 million of that was a veto of future prison construction. Within two years, Clements would have to put prisoners in tents to alleviate prison overcrowding; this became a potent campaign issue in his later challenge from Attorney General Mark White. White questioned the constitutionality of some of the vetoes. The result was that after Clements left office, White eventually restored $90 million of Clements's spending cuts.

Clements brought in a few dollar-a-year men to help run his administration. Among these were his appointments secretary, Tobin Armstrong, a prominent businessman and rancher. Clements's goal was to bring in the best and brightest to serve in appointed positions in the state. In this area, Clements made an immediate impact. As Jim Francis recalls, rural Texas was staunchly Democratic when Clements was elected: "Areas today that vote 80 percent Republican were voting 80 percent Democrat. Clements started a transformation to make Texas first a two-party state, and then a Republican-dominated state. It's a defining period, and Clements is due enormous credit for his ability to communicate with rural Texas to politically change the landscape."[22] Because this transformation that Clements brought about was such a startling departure from deep-seated Texas traditions, Francis elaborates upon just how Clements succeeded in turning overwhelmingly Democratic areas into Republican strongholds: "How did Clements do it? He made a whole bunch of judicial appointments. There were places where there was no chance of winning, but if a Republican had a chance of winning, somebody was going to run as a Republican if they got the appointment. A few got beat, but by the time Clements left office three years later, we had appointed two to three hundred Republican judges, scattered all across Texas. Once you start breaking up the courthouse in rural Texas, you break up voting patterns and completely change the state."[23]

Clements himself spoke frankly of his partisanship in making appointments, while clearly denying that promoting Republican control overshadowed all other concerns: "My inclination certainly would be to appoint someone who either is now a Republican, who will declare as a Republican, or who can get elected as a Republican. But, on the other hand, I'm sure not going to sacrifice quality for that. Quality comes first."[24]

Clements worked to change the political landscape of Texas in another way—by cochairing Ronald Reagan's presidential campaign in Texas in 1980. As he had been when organizing for Nixon in 1972, Clements was fully engaged in Reagan's election efforts. Clements worked to create an effective, streamlined organization. He called Jimmy Carter a liar, and when asked to expound upon that charge, Clements called Carter a "God-damned liar." Reagan responded to Clements's staunch support by calling Clements his favorite governor. Clements was determined to deliver Texas for Reagan in a big way. However, that was not his only goal. As an inside advisor to Reagan, Clements counseled against the briefly popular notion of asking Gerald Ford, the former president, to join the ticket as vice president. Instead, Clements lobbied successfully for the selection of his friend George H. W. Bush. Texans would be inclined to vote for a Texan. With this election, Texas began a radical change.

Because Clements was determined to change Texas into a state in which the Republican Party was significant or even dominant, he opened and staffed a political office, the Governor Clements Committee. It was the first time any Texas officeholder had kept an ongoing political operation open year-round. Jim Francis ran it, and Karl Rove worked there. Recalls Francis:

> Every time there was a special election, we'd go into full campaign mode, and we would recruit the candidate and run the campaign. We knocked off Babe Schwartz [a state senator from Galveston], and we knocked off several incumbents. And we went to a senator from Dallas and tried to convince him to switch parties, and when he didn't, we got him beat in a primary.[25] We made that Democratic seat a Republican seat, and we started doing that all over Texas. Once you start winning elections, it changes the way people think about how they vote. It was a revolutionary time in Texas politics and laid the seeds for Phil Gramm's changing parties, resigning, and running.[26] It started a process that ended up changing this state forever.[27]

In addition, Bill Clements was changing. He knew that during the first legislative session, he had not worked well with the people who could make or break his legislative agenda. The second legislative session would be different. He was better prepared and eager to work with the lawmakers. He had learned from his mistakes. Clements made it a point to work more closely with Speaker Billy Clayton and Lieutenant Governor Bill Hobby. He invited members of the legislature to his office for late-afternoon drinks and frequently had lunch with key legislators. Two years earlier, he had barely won the election. Nevertheless, he began the second legislative session having orchestrated Reagan's notable victory in Texas.

Before the session, Clements appointed some high-profile task forces to look at the issues of education, crime, and drugs. He would base his legislative program upon these issues. He appointed Dallas billionaire Ross Perot to head the War on Drugs task force, which focused on the flow of illegal drugs through Texas. In addition, Clements persuaded Dr. Willis Tate, the former president of Southern Methodist University, to head a task force on public education. This committee helped generate Clements's back-to-basics education agenda. David Dean, a young attorney on Clements's staff, headed a task force on criminal-justice issues.[28]

Addressing the Sixty-seventh Legislature, Clements took a respectful tone in pointing out the long service of several legislators: he called them by name, recounted the years of service of each, and thanked them for their service to the state. He saluted the new members. Clements would advance forty-four items that legislative session and pass all but ten. All but two of the sixteen key elements in his anticrime and War on Drugs package became law. He had learned from his mistakes and had become more skillful at advancing his agenda. Legislators noticed the change and were therefore more willing to work with him.

The economy was good. Businesses were moving to Texas. Clements's increased penalties for various crimes brought about a reduction in crime, reversing a previous negative trend. He sought and got a 23 percent increase in spending for public education, and public school teachers received a pay increase of 26 percent, the highest increase in ten years. Of more than 1,600 appointments submitted to the Senate for confirmation, only four were rejected, including the appointment of Karl Rove, who lacked a college degree, as a university trustee. In all, Clements would make some four thousand appointments, the quality of which he would call the hallmark of his administration.

One of the great challenges of that legislative session stemmed from a prisoner lawsuit called *Ruiz v. Estelle* (1972). In 1980, Judge William Wayne Justice decreed that aspects of the Texas prison system were unconstitutional, particularly overcrowding. To deal with this issue, Clements asked the legislature to appropriate $35 million in emergency funds to build new prison dormitories. This came on the heels of the governor's recent line-item veto of some $30 million in prison-construction funds. In addition, Clements proposed that a compound of army tents be used to house prisoners, since they sufficed for the Texas National Guard troops. His fights on this issue—in particular with Mark White, his attorney general—became fodder for the press. In the end, in compliance with the federal court order, approximately $160 million was budgeted for new prison construction to relieve overcrowding.

In addition to legislative successes, Governor Clements began several initiatives beyond the purview of lawmakers. He made twenty visits to work with the Mexican president and Mexican governors to ensure that a dialogue took place on border initiatives, crime, and other issues of mutual concern. With Mrs. Clements, he led an effort to restore—with private money—the nation's fourth-oldest governor's mansion and to redecorate it in a way that was in keeping with both its historical significance and its contemporary role. Finally, by executive order, Governor Clements created a long-term planning project called Texas 2000, which would identify future needs of the state in all areas.

Looking ahead to the sesquicentennial celebration of statehood in 1986, Clements appointed a commission to plan for the celebration, with a view to attracting tourism and increasing appreciation for the state's unique history. Furthermore, Clements wanted people outside Texas to know what he knew. Because Clements loved Texas history and owned one of the finest collections of books on the subject in the world, he wanted people the world over to learn of the state's past. Toward that end, he arranged a meeting at the Clements's Virginia estate, Wexford, which had been owned by John and Jacqueline Kennedy, with the novelist James Michener. In a letter to the author, Clements asked Michener to write "the story of Texas." Clements's passion comes through in the letter:

> Texas is a story so big, so diverse, that its telling must be by an author who works in comfort with its size and scope. The story of Texas can only be told by someone who has demonstrated that he possesses the vision necessary to capture the vastness of the State and is not intimidated by a vast span of time.
>
> Texans, more so than any other state's citizens, feel something special about their state. This may be due to the vast catalogue of her famous sons. I also believe that this feeling has its strength in the diverse cultural heritage of our land. Texas was and is today a "melting pot" of various cultures and nationalities. Many characterize Texans as being one breed—Maverick.
>
> The story of Texas can be woven from fabric abundant with adventure, heroic action, and decisive leadership. Texas's strong foundation has been reinforced over the 150 years by the actions of powerful leaders and rugged individuals whose foresight knew no boundaries.[29]

After the meeting, Michener agreed. He came to Austin, where he spent thirty months working on the new project. He was given office space and support at the University of Texas. The result was the thousand-page novel *Texas*, which would captivate a worldwide audience.

Clements had become a good governor. He had grown to love the job, and reveled in the history of the state and his role in it. He had a long string of accomplishments. With the management of Reagan's Texas campaign, Clements had learned how to "get out the vote" better than most professional campaign operatives. It was time to begin the campaign for a second term. However, despite his formidable and sharpened political skills, Clements would lose this campaign to his nemesis, Attorney General Mark White.

6

MARK WHITE

And Perot [and White] took on the greatest power in all of Texas: football. The trouble with Texas schools, said Perot, is too much football. Pretty much the whole state flat fell down on hearing such heresy, bewildered as a goat on AstroTurf. The widespread consensus in Texas was that schools exist primarily to support football. Here Ross Perot up and proposed no-pass/no-play. If you don't pass all your courses in school, you can't play football. People were astounded, and it upset the coaches. In Texas politics, it is not wise to upset the coaches.

MOLLY IVINS AND LOU DUBOSE, *Shrub: The Short but Happy Political Life of George W. Bush*

Governor White credits the advancements made in public education during his tenure to the lessons that his mother (a teacher) taught him.

IN 1973, GOVERNOR Dolph Briscoe appointed Mark White, a young, unknown Houston attorney, as secretary of state. Within ten years, he had been elected governor. First, White successfully ran for attorney general, defeating future U.S. treasury secretary and secretary of state James Baker. Four years later, he successfully ran for governor, defeating the incumbent, Governor Bill Clements.

In recalling his political start as Briscoe's secretary of state, White notes: "Not many people expected Briscoe to win the election. Most people thought that Ben Barnes was going to win; the others who didn't like Barnes were from the more liberal part of the party, and they thought that Sissy Farenthold ought to win. Those who were left over were for Briscoe, and I was part of the ones left over. I don't know that he had a very large pool to pick from."[1] In his first run at elective office, White became attorney general after defeating Price Daniel, Jr., in the primary. As political observer Paul Burka noted:

> White was a mediocre attorney general, especially when judged against John Hill, the man he succeeded. Hill, using his considerable reputation as a trial lawyer to lure talent from the State's top law firms, assembled a first-rate law office. White promptly dismantled it. Some of Hill's best people fled; others got the boot, causing more to flee. Lacking Hill's professional credentials, White couldn't recruit equivalent replacements. Nor was he an administrator; on more than one occasion, his lawyers failed to show up for trials, resulting in cases lost by default.
>
> In big cases, White won about as often as the Houston Rockets. He sued Montana over its rapacious 30-percent coal severance tax, which is passed along to Texas customers. He lost. He defended the State prison system, and again he lost.[2]

It seemed unlikely that his political career would advance. He had a poor record as attorney general. He was disliked by both Governor Clements and the powerful comptroller, Bob Bullock. Carolyn Barta writes that from the start there was friction between Clements and White. Almost as soon as White took office as attorney general, "he began talking to reporters about running for governor. Clements said later that he and White clashed because of White's ambitions and 'because of his mental deficiencies. He was a lightweight.' But the two also had a different view of White's role. The governor thought that the attorney general should be the governor's lawyer; White viewed his job as the State's lawyer, even if it meant crossing the governor."[3]

This differing view of the role of attorney general was highlighted in the first year of the new governor's term when a major oil blowout in the Bay of Campeche eventually dumped 3.3 million barrels of oil into the Gulf of Mexico. The oil rig involved was owned by Clements's company, SEDCO, although SEDCO was not the operator of the rig. The spill threatened the Texas coast and had environmental groups and others quite exercised, but Clements downplayed the disaster as "a big to-do about nothing" and described the event as not serious. Two weeks later, oil slicks covered almost all of the beaches from Port Aransas to the Rio Grande: "Tourist occupancy on the Texas coast was down fifty percent at the peak of the season, and business losses were estimated in the millions of dollars."[4] When White called a press conference and criticized the governor's "big to-do about nothing" stance, the first volley, insofar as Clements was concerned, had been fired. White recalls that the big oil spill precipitated a rift: Clements "made the unfortunate statements: 'All it takes is a big hurricane to take care of that problem' and 'Don't worry about it.' Then he really got mad when I went out and sued him. The biggest oil spill in the world to date hits the Texas coast, and he took that personally! I tried to tell him that I've got to do this. The politics are that you've *got* to do it. If you didn't, somebody would rightfully oust you from office."[5]

As the lawyer for all state agencies, White felt that he had to do more. He solicited input from Texas oil companies and environmental groups to determine what more could be done to respond to oil-spill emergencies. Carolyn Barta writes that Clements, furious, wrote a letter in which he accused "White of impugning the oil-spill recovery actions taken by the governor's office, the U.S. Coast Guard, the National Oceanic and Atmospheric Administration, the Environmental Protection Agency, and six different State departments or agencies."[6]

Clements believed that White had overstepped his authority, as he made clear in a memorandum to White:

> As you are no doubt aware, your entry into this area is without constitutional or statutory authority. It serves only to confuse and mislead the public and those agencies and officials responsible for crisis management of this nature. Further, your refusal of my personal request to allow my general counsel, David Dean, and Frank Cox, the coordinator of Disaster Emergency Services, to attend the meeting clearly calls into question your motives and intentions in this matter.[7]

Clearly, Clements and White clashed head-on over this environmental disaster, which led many pundits to ponder why they viewed the crisis so differently. Clements's press aide, Reggie Bashur, con-

First Lady Rosalynn Carter addresses the state senate, 1984.

cludes that two very different men simply were wired to react to events such as the environmental spill very differently. In part, this was easy to understand, given that Clements had a background as a drilling contractor, so he knew the dreary fact that spills are bound to occur. To him, this was just a problem to be solved, a mess to be cleaned up, not something that lent itself to histrionic accusations. According to Bashur, Clements was not "callous to the environment or protective of anything. Instead, when there was a problem, Clements would want to step back, deliberate, come up with an answer, and methodically, quietly get it fixed. He didn't like to grandstand. He did not want to shout from the rafters, 'I feel your pain.' He just wanted to say, 'We've got a problem—let's resolve it.' Clements was a workhorse. White was a show horse."[8]

White soon knew that he would challenge Clements for the governorship. He recalls that his wife, Linda Gale, helped him reach that decision, even though practically everyone else urged him to wait until after Clements's (presumed) second term. As White remembers it, one morning his wife told him, "You know, I think we'd be better off if you ran for governor and were defeated than to run for reelection for attorney general and get elected and have to serve four more years with this guy."[9] He agreed. However, White first had to win the Democratic primary.

Also in the race were Texas land commissioner Bob Armstrong, who was popular with the press, and another former legislator, Buddy Temple, the son of an East Texas timber baron and vice chairman of Time, Inc. Temple, who had been elected to the Texas Railroad Commission in 1981, was the most serious challenger to White and was not afraid to challenge White's mediocre record as attorney general, calling him the "Edsel of the attorney generals" and the "Pinocchio of Texas politics."[10] Temple borrowed over a million dollars to run his primary campaign.

For his part, White focused more on Clements than on his primary foes. In something of a lackluster primary fight, White led the group, with 45 percent of the vote, but he failed to win the majority needed to avoid a runoff. Temple followed, with 30 percent of the vote, while Armstrong ran a distant third. Realizing that a continued primary fight would cost each candidate another million dollars and leave the nominee somewhat damaged before the main fight with Governor Clements, Buddy Temple withdrew, giving White the Democratic Party's nomination. Both White and Clements wanted this outcome. Both were braced for the fight. As Clements told the *Dallas Times Herald* on May 8, 1982, "You might say I've been licking my chops for three years."[11]

Clements had a well-funded campaign and the endorsements of three former governors: Shivers, Smith, and Connally. All three joined Clements at a fund-raiser in Houston at which the keynote speakers were President Reagan and Vice President Bush. While the campaign of any Democratic challenger against an incumbent Republican governor would be tough, Texas was still voting overwhelmingly in the Democratic column. In the recent primary, some 1.3 million voters participated in the Democratic primary, while only 265,000 cast votes in the Republican primary. Democrats controlled both houses of the legislature.

The campaign was conducted fiercely on both sides. When asked by a reporter why voters should support him, Clements replied: "I am competent, and he's incompetent."[12] Former attorneys general Will Wilson, John Ben Shepperd, Waggoner Carr, and Gerald Mann endorsed Clements.

The Clements campaign printed a flyer called "The Texas Spectator" and mailed it to 1.5 million Texans. This flyer details the story of White's arrest in Athens, Texas, as a twenty-three-year-old Baylor law student. While drinking and driving, White crashed his Volkswagen into a parked car. A driving-while-intoxicated charge was reduced to a charge of public intoxication, and White was given a fifty-dollar fine. Although the incident had occurred approximately two decades before the race, Clements felt justified in using the derogatory information against his opponent in the campaign. White was able to turn this to his advantage, however, since the public seemed more willing to forgive the youthful indiscretion than the ruthless tactics of the state's chief executive.

Another blow to the Clements campaign came when a small-town newspaper asked the governor whether he would consider appointing a minority or a housewife to a vacant spot on the Public Utility Commission. Clements said that he did not know of any housewife qualified to sit on the board. In elaborating on the subject, he stated that the appointee should be familiar with the utilities industries and the intricacies of bonded indebtedness. When Democrats used this statement against Clements, they changed "housewife" to "woman," portraying Clements as an out-of-date male chauvinist.

In many ways, the race became a referendum on the personality of Bill Clements. With every charge made by White, Clements became irritable and lashed out in personal attacks at White. Albert Hunt of the *Wall Street Journal* described Governor Clements as abrasive and unwilling to admit mistakes, even after being reminded of the surge in support that President Kennedy received after taking responsibility for the botched Bay of Pigs operation against Fidel Castro. Clements's response to that was characteristically combative: "'Well, I don't have any Bay of Pigs,' he snaps. 'And I didn't drive any girl off a bridge either.'[13] This is vintage Bill Clements: blunt, bull-headed, tactless, tough, and mean. This is the way he became Texas's first Republican governor since Reconstruction. This is the way he has behaved for the past four years, and this is the way he is running for reelection."[14]

Although Clements clearly had the edge in campaign funding, White benefited from the simultaneous reelection efforts of Senator Lloyd Bentsen and Lieutenant Governor Bill Hobby. Both of them were very popular, and both were being challenged by weak opponents. With their resources pooled for phone banks and get-out-the-vote efforts, White's ability to reach his base found new legs.

White believed that rising utility rates were an issue that resonated with the average voter. His polls justified that conclusion. However, Governor Clements continued to think that the whole utility issue was of little consequence. Further stoking the idea that Clements was out of touch, Clements responded to the utility-rate discussion by saying, "People are just going to have to conserve more. When I grew up, there was no air conditioning, and we got along fine."[15] However, White's future chief of staff, Pike Powers, argues that it was more than polling that spurred White to grab and run with this utility issue. White had great empathy for consumers and the effect of this issue on them, "and he could play a crowd on that issue better than anybody else I've seen. He knew exactly when to bring it up and how to pump it and hit the right nerves at the right moment."[16]

Governor White and agriculture commissioner Jim Hightower planting vegetables on the mansion grounds, 1984.

Each candidate had formidable advantages, and these were quite evenly balanced, so the race was tight. Apparently, the race was much closer than the strategists in the Clements campaign realized. Mark White recalls that going into Election Day, his polls showed an even race, but the Clements's campaign seemed to see things differently. Nevertheless, White chose to use his characteristic campaign strategy of running on the issues rather than resorting to attack ads. He attributes the intensity of his support to that approach: "That's what got people out to vote on what turned out to be a rainy day for Election Day for governor in '82. It was flooding on the west side of San Antonio, and people ran out of ballots in Houston, with people standing in the rain to vote. Dallas was similar. Voters were energized, and they stayed out and voted."[17] Carolyn Barta writes that Clements's advisor Jack Rains realized that the Clements campaign was in jeopardy "when he drove the black precincts and found people standing in line, in the rain, to vote. He reported to campaign headquarters in Austin, 'These people are motivated. They're mad. We're in deep shit.'"[18]

This realization came too late to be of any use to the Clements campaign. Mark White won handily, with 53.2 percent to Clements's 46 percent. Of the more than 3.1 million votes cast, White collected 1,697,870 to Clements's 1,465,937. Clements had spent approximately $12 million, twice as much as his challenger, but to no avail.

White now had to govern. Before he was sworn into office, he found himself in the middle of a significant controversy over the outgoing governor's prerogative of making "midnight appointments." Defeated governors, with a century of tradition and constitutional authority on their side, have made appointments after their defeat. At issue were some one hundred appointments made by Clements. White felt that Clements was conspiring to name people who were hostile to White and his agenda. The perception that the new governor was seeking to "bust" these traditional midnight appointees for political purposes was pervasive. Commenting at the time on White's presumed attempt to block these appointments, Clements said, "There will be scars and wounds and hard feelings that will come out of this that are totally unnecessary."[19] Among those appointments were popular high-profile persons, including former governor John Connally and former Speaker Bill Clayton. Pike Powers recalls how White asked Clements to rescind his "midnight appointments":

> Most people said Clements was doing it to be mean-spirited and to embarrass White. I, on the other hand, thought that Clements was trying to expand the power of the gubernatorial office in an appropriate way. We thought we had persuaded White to ask for some of the appointments back, but not all of them. I mean, for example, let John Connally stay on the University of Texas Board of Regents, and let Speaker Clayton stay on the A&M Board of Regents. Let's not disturb those fights; just let those go. But there was a guy named Lloyd Doggett who went in and saw White that morning. He was a state senator. And he said you must in the name of the Democratic Party—if you are ever going to get anything done—you have to ask for all of them back.[20]

Powers considers White's request that Clements rescind all the appointments "the most damaging thing that happened to him."[21]

White himself looks back on that controversy with some regret. He admits that what he probably feels worst about is its effect on former governor Connally, even though White did not mention Connally specifically when he sent the list of all of Clements's appointments to the Senate for a vote: "Larry Temple [Connally's former chief aide] gave me good advice that I didn't take. But Connally was rejected by the largest number of votes in the Senate of anybody who had been rejected, only because he changed parties. At that time, the Democratic Party had about twenty-five votes, and you had the more liberal senators grinding their teeth to get at Connally. I should not have let that happen."[22] As one unnamed lobbyist said at the time concerning the appointee recall: "There's going to be enough blood coming out from under those closed Senate doors to flood the press room across the rotunda."[23]

Governor White also faced unusual fiscal challenges in his governorship. In his first address to the legislature, he boasted of the sound finances of Texas, which had no budget deficit, unlike forty-one other states at the time: "According to the latest State comptroller's estimate, we will have twenty-one percent more money to spend for the '84/'85 biennium—over four billion dollars in new revenues. The issue before us is how we are to set priorities in allocating this new revenue among competing demands. Our task is not to decide where to cut. Our task is to decide wisely where to spend."[24]

However, Lieutenant Governor Hobby, as chairman of the Legislative Budget Board, estimated a $5.1 billion spending shortfall for the biennium and predicted that only $1.5 billion from the existing surplus would be available to compensate for it.[25]

The world for Mark White and for Texas changed quickly. Oil prices dropped by two-thirds—disastrous in a state overly reliant upon tax revenues from oil. In his second address to the legislature, less than two years later, the governor addressed the new fiscal reality: "The recent recession and plummeting tax revenues from oil and gas have left our state in a financial bind. If we continue business as usual, our spending would exceed our income by $791 million during the next two years."[26]

In hindsight, the stark but unanticipated drop in the price of oil had huge budget implications for Texas. In reflecting upon this drastic change, White recalls that the price for a barrel of oil plummeted from $26–28 when he took office to a low of $9 a barrel in 1986: "Every dollar it went down, annualized, cost the state a billion dollars. So you've got to see that the percentage of our state budget revenues were about 22 percent from oil and gas when I took office, but when I left office, it was less than 10 percent."[27] Because of this decline in tax revenues from oil, White says that he had to raise other taxes.

On the day that White was elected, Comptroller Bob Bullock announced that he would run for governor in 1986. During White's first legislative session, Bullock lowered his state revenue estimate by more than three billion dollars. (By law, the Texas legislature can spend no more than the comptroller estimates that it will have over the two-year spending period.)

However, despite these difficulties, White's tenure was marked by accomplishments. In his address to the legislature, he called for a "catch up" pay raise for public school teachers. By the end of the second special session of the legislature, minimum teacher salaries had been increased from $4,100 to $15,200. He called for increased funding for bilingual education, and he got it. Famously, these and other changes came about because of White's appointing of Dallas billionaire H. Ross Perot to chair his Select Committee on Public Education. After holding hearings around the state on matters of school finance, teacher compensation, curriculum, and extracurricular activities, the committee's report became the basis for the wide-ranging education reforms in House Bill 72. The gap between the richest and the poorest school districts was significantly narrowed. Student-teacher ratios were lowered, and a "no-pass, no-play" dictum was delivered with regard to extracurricular activities.

White attributes the makeup of the comprehensive reforms to what his school-teaching mother had taught him: "Everything in House Bill 72 is a result of what my mother said when she came home from school. She taught the first grade. She said, 'I've got too many kids, and they aren't ready for school. They don't have enough money for school supplies.' She had to take her own money and buy school supplies. I've got pictures of her classroom in the first grade with thirty-four kids in it."[28] Obviously, this issue of excessively large class sizes had struck White from an early age. As White explains, "We had a state law back then of having twenty-eight kids average per classroom. *Aver-*

*HRH Charles, the Prince of Wales, visits the
Governor's Mansion, 1986.*

age is a wonderful word, and you'll notice it is not in House Bill 72.
They wanted it in there. I said no. Hard limit, exceptions only for
hardship. It will hurt some, but it will mostly help. My mother said,
'I don't have a duty-free lunch period.' You do now! We passed a bill
for it."[29]

In higher education, White called for the enactment of a constitu-
tional amendment to create a construction fund for non–Permanent
University Fund schools and to expand the Permanent University
Fund to cover all University of Texas and Texas A&M institutions.[30]
The legislature adopted a joint resolution for these purposes.

With utility reform as the hallmark of his campaign, White sought
to reorganize the Public Utility Commission by having its members
be elected by popular vote instead of appointed by the governor, the
practice at the time. This would also serve to deflect consumer criticism of the governor for rate hikes. However, he failed to anticipate

the opposition in the legislature to this proposal, which would ultimately doom it.

White further pledged to appoint a housewife to the panel. White's chief of staff, Pike Powers, recalls that after a lunch with White at a Mexican restaurant that included "several margaritas," the press swarmed around them as they walked back to the capitol "because two of Clements's appointees to the Public Utility Commission had offered their resignations that day. White didn't know. And they asked: 'What are you going to do to fill the position that you promised to a housewife?' And he said: 'By God, I'll have it by sunset.' It was the margaritas talking! We had to scare up appointees by sunset. I was on the phone for hours doing due diligence on whether this person was really able and looking at integrity issues. *I'll have it done by sunset!*"[31]

White's political instincts served him well: replacements were lined up by the end of the day. Although critics claimed that White had overpromised by stating that he would find a qualified housewife for the post, he proved them wrong. His appointment of Peggy Rosson, a housewife who had served on the El Paso Utility Board, met with widespread approval.

However, White could get no traction within the legislature to advance his notion that the members of the Public Utility Commission (PUC) should be elected. In an unprecedented step, White bought television time and took his case to the people. As Paul Burka writes, "The TV spots made it seem as if he were still a candidate, not a governor; still seeking popular approval instead of operating on the inside; still acting for his own good, not the public's."[32] White's use of this tactic with other issues earned him the nickname "Media Mark."

Although unsuccessful in bringing about an elected PUC, White had other successes. The legislature created and funded an office of general counsel, independent of the PUC, to advocate for the consumer. Utility rates were lowered, and the ability of utility companies to claim price hikes because of automatic fuel adjustments was ended.

White instituted a dynamic change in the way the legislature and the governor's office worked together. According to Dave McNeely in the *Austin American-Statesman*, Clements was bossy and ineffective with the legislature during his first two years, but became much more effective in the second half of his term. Under White, "Texas had a governor who lacked an extensive legislative program, a new House speaker whose primary goal was to stop new taxes, and a taciturn, businesslike lieutenant governor who directed what was probably the most competent, intelligent, efficient, and dull Senate in recent history."[33] Although White failed to get his elected PUC, and it took a special session for his education reforms and teacher pay increases to come about, significant legislation was passed in the areas of mental health, prison reform, and utility regulation. At a press conference on June 1, 1983, White outlined the successful legislative accomplishments of his administration as he saw them: "I think that you will find the criminal justice system package and the major overhaul in parks and wildlife regulation, as well as in mental health and mental retardation, signify a major overhaul. We've restructured the Texas Industrial Commission in a way that will attract new industry to our state. And I believe that if we'd done nothing else except getting MCC [Microelectronics and Computer Technology Corporation] to come to Texas, then we would have had a very successful 140 days here."[34]

In a special session, White broke his campaign pledge and signed a $4.8 billion tax bill, which helped buy the education reforms, including the teacher pay raise. Nonetheless, many teachers were incensed over a provision that required them to pass a one-time literacy test to remain employed. And coaches were outraged over the no-pass–no-play provision, which kept students from participating in extracurricular activities if they were not making good grades. Recalls White: "I was frankly surprised at the intensity of the resistance that came from the football coaches, but I've come to learn otherwise as far as rural Texas is concerned. One of my security guys said, 'Governor, we are going to let you have our guns when you go out to West Texas.'"[35] Despite his initial surprise at this vehemently negative reaction, White was quick to take responsibility for his decision and the firestorm that erupted in the wake of his policy. As he readily admits, "I had single-handedly made the schoolteachers mad, and I can't blame anyone else. They asked me if I wanted to give the teachers their raise before or after they took the test. I said to give it to them now. Big mistake! What I should have done was let them qualify for the money by passing the test. They had long forgotten the money by the time the test came along, but they remembered me, and we offended a lot of teachers and coaches."[36]

In his address at the next legislative session, White acknowledged the fiscal bind that the state was in, adding that though one option was to raise taxes, no one, himself included, intended to do so. The other option: "We can tighten our belts and bring our spending levels down to our income levels. And that is exactly what we are going to do. And I believe that we can do it without major disruptions, undue hardships, layoffs, or governmental chaos."[37]

With his poll numbers down and teacher groups antagonized, White approached the legislative session with considerable caution. The legislature passed his proposals to increase tuition for most college students threefold, double the price of automobile license plates, and raise most state fees. Former state senator Ray Farabee complained to the *Austin American-Statesman* that many people were diligently trying to devise a way to fund those programs without raising taxes, but White's only proposal was to pay "for everything by increasing court costs."[38]

White called for a well-planned water strategy. The legislature passed and sent to the voters a constitutional amendment that encouraged conservation and provided for a low-cost means of financing future water needs, but the legislature failed to support White's initiatives to increase the number of officers in the Department of Public Safety and the creation of an antiracketeering statute aimed at organized crime.

By 1986, with the Texas economy in a recession, White called the legislature into special session to make deeper budget cuts and to enact a $763 million tax bill, which he signed. It was only two months before the election, and White told legislators to blame him. Everyone did.

With all of this considerable political baggage, Mark White entered the 1986 election. However, in a contemporary piece, Paul Burka notes: "The incumbent is a likable person, well-meaning and sincere. The record of his four years in office—unprecedented advances in public education, water development, and indigent health care—ranks with the best administrations in Texas history. His tenure is free of scandal. He looks good on television. In the course of his political ascendancy, he has vanquished some of the biggest names in

Texas politics. Now he is running against a man he has already beaten once, a sixty-nine-year-old former governor with a modest record and a penchant for mean-spirited remarks."[39] Despite the budget problems and political flak that White faced while seeking reelection, he had many things for which he could take credit and from which he could gain support.

7

WILLIAM P. CLEMENTS'S SECOND TERM

A serial letter writer gets a Bullock "drive-by ass chewing":

March 23, 1987

Dear Mr. _____:

After three years of glorious silence, you have reared your old sore head again.

I'd like to get my hands on whomever kicked over that rock and let you out again.

Every time you write me one of your nut letters, you remind me that you were in World War II. If that's true, I wonder how we ever won the war. Maybe that's why it took so long. Which side were you on?

You also remind me that you were a rice farmer and a cattleman. Maybe you were, but if you had an ounce of decency about you, you would keep that quiet out of respect for the decent people who have been in the same business.

I've never believed in an income tax, but I'll be damned if I wouldn't support one if I thought it would run you out of Texas.

As a public official, I get irrational letters such as yours from time to time. We don't particularly worry about any one of them. However, when they develop a pattern such as yours have over the years, criminologists and those trained in behavioral sciences advise that caution is in order, as this pattern has potential for violence.

That being the case, notification of the proper authorities is in order as a preventative measure to deter possible harm to innocent bystanders. I hope the family will understand the necessity of such.

Sincerely,
Bob Bullock
Comptroller of Public Accounts

William P. Clements, 1982. "I don't think he gave two tinkers' damn for one millisecond what people thought," said Jim Francis.

KENT HANCE defeated George W. Bush in 1978 to win his seat in Congress. Former congressman Hance and Congressman Tom Loeffler were lining up backers for their respective primary bids to be the Republican nominee for governor. Beginning immediately after his reelection loss in 1982, Bill Clements had adamantly denied any interest in running again. He had sold his company, SEDCO, to Schlumberger Limited for $1.2 billion. He was sixty-eight years old.

Assured that Clements would not consider a run, Karl Rove went to work for Kent Hance, taking charge of the direct-mail campaign, while Jim Francis agreed to manage Hance's effort. Hance had lost a Democratic primary runoff for the U.S. Senate in 1984, and switched to the Republican Party in 1985 to run for governor. "Gee, I miss Gov. Clements" bumper stickers showed up on bumpers statewide. Several friends and supporters tried to get Clements to change his mind, but to no avail. However, on a campaign trip to East Texas in support of congressional candidate Edd Hargett, Clements got the wind back in his sails. The improbable place in which he announced to the press his intention to run again was at a urinal in a men's room at a small airport, where he ran into *Dallas Morning News* political writer Sam Attlesey. "Attlesey asked the governor, 'Are you going to run again?' Clements responded, 'I think I am. Rita and I were talking about it last night.' At a press conference in Marshall, he said, 'Rita and I are seriously considering whether we should make this race.' He told Attlesey he was 'ninety-five percent certain.' Attlesey wrote the story."[1] Clements said that he felt that Mark White was not the kind of person who should be governor and that neither of the two congressmen could put together a successful effort to defeat him.

The next day, at a quickly thrown-together press conference at Dallas's Union Station, Clements became the first announced candidate in the Republican primary. Rove recused himself from the Hance campaign to go back to work for his mentor. However, others did not follow Rove's lead. Clements began phoning his previous supporters, many of whom had already committed to other candidates, including Jim Francis; appointments secretary Tobin Armstrong; Bum Bright, an A&M regent appointed by Clements; and pollster Lance Tarrance. Following his announcement, Bill and Rita Clements left for a month-long fishing expedition in Alaska, which they had planned months in advance, leaving the campaign with no manager, no organized sup-port, and no finance director.

However, when Clements returned, he hired Reggie Bashur as his press assistant and a television crew selected specifically to take the rough edges off the candidate. Clements easily won the primary race without a runoff, with 58 percent of the vote, even carrying Congress-man Loeffler's home district. Clements was ready to take on Governor White, whom Clements had taken to referring to as "the governor of Taxes."

White's timing was bad. He had assumed office at a time when the economy was petroleum-driven, but during his tenure, crude oil prices plummeted from over $26 a barrel to under $9 a barrel. Dallas and Houston led the nation in office vacancies, and corporate bank-ruptcies increasingly infected the business community. Unemploy-ment at times exceeded 10 percent. The legislature was forced to raise sales and gasoline taxes just months before the election. White told legislators to tell folks that he was to blame. They did—and so did Bill Clements. Mark White was down in the polls. He confesses that at first, although only his wife knew this, he did not intend to seek reelection: "I had pretty much done everything that I wanted to do. There were two or three other things that I had to do. But I ran for re-election for the wrong reasons. I didn't think Bill Clements ought to be the governor of Texas. I did not think that it would be good for Texas, and that's why I ran."[2] However, in January 1986, the polls were so lopsidedly in Clements's favor—thirty points—that neither campaign even mentioned them, "because nobody would believe it, but by the time the election came around the last week, I felt like we were going to win. I didn't have that feeling like I did the first time. We got back, and our polls showed us ahead on Sunday before the election on Tues-day by one or two points."[3]

However, despite the turn of events that suggested that White had become the embodiment of one of America's most beloved archetypes, the comeback kid, and was about to snatch victory from what had seemed like a crushing defeat, the miraculous recovery and reversal of fortune collapsed. As he recalls, "Then, all the evangelicals on Sunday papered all the cars over East Texas, and our polls started slipping then. I think I won by a quarter of a million votes the first time and lost by a quarter million the second time."[4]

So why did he go down to defeat after coming so close to pulling off an upset? Apparently, the "governor of Taxes" label had gained some political traction, among other things. White has pondered the reasons, which he sees as including teachers' anger over the testing requirement, coaches' anger over the no-pass–no-play rule, and widespread anger over his decision to raise taxes. White stresses that although he was accused of lying about taxes, he had never promised that he would not raise taxes: "The *Fort Worth Star-Telegram* said there'll be no need for any new taxes in my term, but they didn't read my statement before that. I'd said that if everything stays as it is now, there will be no need for any new taxes. So they just cut out that phrase and said look at all the taxes I'd raised. Hell, I'd raised everything. I raised taxes on everything across the board!"[5]

Against the backdrop of these economic problems, White bought a $3.1 million Mitsubishi jet. Pike Powers explains the reasoning behind White's decision, which might have seemed frivolous or self-indulgent at a time that called for economic belt-tightening: "Mitsubishi had its facility in San Angelo, and as an economic-development governor, White really believed that it was important to support the platform of an aircraft manufacturer in Texas. And here are the Japanese, who have decided to put a fairly significant investment in Texas. He really wanted to support that. And in his heart, he was doing that."[6]

However, the economic-development angle was not the only legitimate reason for the purchase of the jet; safety was also a real concern. As Powers notes, "It sounded a little thin when you talked about the prior plane. It was barely flyable. White got paranoid about close calls and bad equipment with bad pilots. His thinking was, 'I'm the chief executive officer of this state, and I'm entitled to safety.' He saw the Mitsubishi jet as a way to upgrade the safety. I'm not sure how the average voter felt about it, but the combination of safety and economic development of Texas with a plane made in San Angelo was enough to persuade him that it was worth the political risk."[7]

White had rolled the dice, and the gamble ended up paying off for his opponent. The Clements team found that, in addition to problems with the economy and job creation, White's purchase of the state-owned Japanese jet polled very well to Clements's benefit. Although White started with a terrible deficit in polling numbers, he success-fully reduced that disadvantage and turned the race into a tight one. The two camps agreed to a televised debate. Reggie Bashur recalls that at the debate, the two candidates did not want to shake hands, but did so for the press: "And so they finally extended hands. Clements says, 'Well, Mark, your cartridge is dry,' and White looked at Clements and said, 'Bill, you ready for business?'"[8]

Bashur recalls that he said to Clements during the debate prep,

> "Why don't we get under White's skin? Let's get him off stride. When you get any kind of question about the budget, segue into that we've got to live within our means and cut waste." I sug-gested that Clements say, "To cut waste, I'll sell the jet." I sug-gested [we] itemize what is in the jet. You could say, "And I'll sell that $500 gold-plated ashtray, and I'll sell that $35,000 carpet, and I'll sell"—fifteen items. I wrote them all out. Clements takes that piece of paper and sticks it in his pocket, and that's the last I hear about it.[9]

Bashur was pleased when this debate preparation paid a big dividend for Clements. The first question to Clements was about balancing the budget by cutting waste: "You could just see it click with Clements. He had a big smile on his face as he pulled the list out of the jacket, and he's got my piece of paper with the items. He doesn't just pick one or two; he reads all fifteen! White got beet red. Clements won the debate. White never got back on track."[10]

This was the costliest governor's race in Texas history up to that point, with White spending $12 million and Clements spending $13 million. It ended with Clements garnering 52.7 percent of the vote—1.8 million votes to White's 1.5 million. There had not been a comeback bid for the governorship since Miriam "Ma" Ferguson had made one fifty years before. Bill Clements would return to the man-sion he had restored during the state's worst fiscal crisis since the Depression.

Just over a week after the election, a news story broke that would cast a dark shadow over Clements's victory. This story involved a foot-ball play-for-pay scandal at Southern Methodist University, where Clements chaired the board of regents. Within thirty days, the president of the university, Donald Shields, resigned, ostensibly for health reasons. By January, the athletic director, the head coach, and the recruiting coordinator had resigned. An in-house probe was ongoing, and it seemed likely that the football program would be abolished. As Reggie Bashur remembers: "Clements was brought back for a second tour of duty to be the head of the SMU board of governors to clean up a mess. He discovered that twenty-six football players were being paid by alumni to play. He phased out the payments. He tried to do no harm to the institution or to the people around it. He didn't want to stand up and act as a demagogue or blow a whistle and attract attention to himself at the expense of other people."[11]

Clements's motives, his reasoning, his judgments, and his actions surrounding his response to the crisis may have been admirable, but reporters did not give Clements credit for how he handled the situation, so this turned into a low point "for the second Clements administration. It did distract the administration early on. Any new administration is going to have a momentum created by the victory and the feeling of newness and freshness, but a lot of that was dampened because of this issue."[12] The electorate was bombarded with stories of Clements's agreement to phase out rather than stop the payments to the athletes immediately. ABC's *Nightline* did a segment on the scandal, and the *New York Times* ran a front-page story on it. According to one account: "Asked by Dave McNeely of the *Austin American-Statesman* if he had given the 'whole truth and nothing but the truth,' Clements finally made one of those unforgettable, quintessential Clements statements. 'Well, you know, we weren't operating like inaugural day, with a Bible, Dave, and there wasn't ever a Bible present.'"[13] At the following week's press conference, a reporter placed a Bible among the microphones on the dais, a sure sign that Clements's attempt at humor—a feeble effort to make light of what many regarded as a travesty of ethics—had backfired. Clements's relations with the press continued to deteriorate. His staff seemed to be in the dumps, and the governor seemed to lack the pep for which he had once been famous.

In the middle of the play-for-pay scandal, and despite a pledge not

Bill Clements and George H. W. Bush, 1982. Clements, Ronald Reagan's
favorite governor, had successfully lobbied for the selection of Bush as the
vice presidential nominee.

to raise taxes, Clements reluctantly agreed to sign a $5.7 billion tax
bill—the largest in Texas history—to avert a financial crisis. The SMU
scandal and the signing of the tax bill undermined his credibility and
his popularity both within and outside the capitol. During his campaign, he vowed to fight "any and all new taxes" and touted a "secret"
budget plan to get the state through its problems. At the conclusion of
the legislative session, Clements had the highest disapproval rating of
any governor since Preston Smith during the Sharpstown stock-fraud
scandal.[14]

However, despite this rocky start to his second term, Clements
would go on to have legislative successes. On the opening day of the
Seventy-first Legislature, Clements stunned lawmakers by doing something out of character: graciously inviting "them and their spouses to
the Governor's Mansion for an elaborate buffet and cocktails, an overt

peace offering—the only time the first Republican governor since Reconstruction had included the Democratic majority in such a gathering. The symbolism was not lost on the politicians."[15]

In addition, Clements appointed former opponents to prominent positions—Kent Hance to the Railroad Commission and Tom Loeffler to the University of Texas Board of Regents. However, as Clements had promised, he would never change his style or who he essentially was. His aide Cliff Johnson says that Clements didn't treat legislators differently based on party affiliation. In any case, "he wanted direct, abrupt what-do-you-want, what-do-you-want-me-to-do, this-is-what-I-believe kind of talk. If you asked him a question, you got an answer. There was no fuzziness. Whether you liked it was not his concern. His concern was making sure that you understood what he said."[16]

Just as he had restored the Governor's Mansion to its former glory, he now focused on the state capitol. A massive hole was dug on the north grounds of the capitol in which to build an underground four-story annex containing two floors of committee rooms and offices for legislators, and two stories of parking. Its pink granite interior would match that of the Renaissance Revival main building. Clements persuaded the legislature to appropriate $161 million for the renovation and construction.

In addition, Clements enjoyed other successes: workers' compensation reform, tort reform, the consolidation of agencies to create the Department of Commerce, and the construction of thirty thousand new prison beds, among other things. The longest-serving governor in Texas history had left his mark. However, at the age of seventy-two, Clements was tired. As he told reporter Ross Ramsey: "Eight years in this job is long enough. You wear out your welcome. You run out of ideas. You run out of freshness of approach. You run out of energy. You just get tired of what you're doing."[17]

8

ANN RICHARDS

The state that Ann Richards presides over is different than the one I governed twenty-five years ago. It will be different ten years from now than it is today. The real question for us in Texas, as a nation, is whether or not we have the insight and the courage to restructure our government in time to meet the changing conditions that will touch each of our individual lives.

JOHN B. CONNALLY, *In History's Shadow*

A Dallas Times Herald headline in 1990: "Richards Wins in a Mudslide."

WHEN ANN RICHARDS first captured the attention of the nation, as the keynote speaker at the 1988 Democratic National Convention, she was the state treasurer of Texas. At the time of the convention, a television reporter asked Richards's father: "'Well, Mr. Willis, when you told your daughter that she could do anything she wanted to do if she just worked hard enough, did you ever dream that she would do this?' Her father replied: 'Hell, I didn't even know there was a this!'"[1] When she was elected treasurer, Richards was the first woman to have been elected to statewide office in Texas in over fifty years. From there, she became the first female governor elected whose husband had not held the job first.[2] As a darling of the press and a friend of Bill Clinton—who would assume the presidency two years into her gubernatorial term—Richards's stature was national in scope.

Like Harry Truman, Richards's first elective office was that of county commissioner. However, in twentieth-century Texas, the commissioner's court was not much of a political steppingstone. When she took office in 1977, 18 women were county commissioners in Texas, along with 997 men. The precinct that she represented had 85,000 constituents, mostly inside the City of Austin, along approximately five hundred miles of streets and roads. As a female elected official in a progressive county at a time when few did what she did, Richards was on the forefront of change. She served on the President's Advisory Committee for Women, spoke at conferences all over the nation, and advocated for causes beyond Precinct 3 on issues that affected many in a significant way. In many ways, she was beginning anew in her midforties, thinking of public office for the first time and rethinking the view she had accepted until then that a woman's role was to be a wife and mother. Despite her comfort with men and the skill with which she interacted with them, she came increasingly into contact with committed feminists: "Especially after she attended a National Women's Educational Fund conference in Aspen, Colorado, in 1978, she was swayed to their point of view. She had never shied from responsibility, but now the decisions that she made helped determine policies that affected thousands of people and the expenditure of millions of tax dollars."[3]

Her political responsibilities beyond Travis County caused her to see a bigger world and to learn what could be possible and how she might cause those possibilities to come to be. Richards's longtime friend and associate, Jane Hickie, recounts, "She was the first and only governor, I believe, that we have ever had who knows how to build a road and could plan highways. If she were sitting here with us today and you were talking about transportation problems in Houston, she could draw the designs of what ought to be done. She has a phenomenal planning and transportation capability."[4]

Once Richards had seen this bigger world and the impact that she could have on it, her inner circle began to discuss the next, bigger stage. In January 1982 the *Austin American-Statesman* reported that subpoenas were being served on the employees of state treasurer Warren G. Harding and that files and papers were being removed from his office; Richards knew what the next step must be. While no indictments had been handed down, it was clear that Travis County district attorney Ronnie Earle was looking into Harding's relationship with bankers, his lack of properly bidding deposits for certain banks, and the improper use of state employees in his election activities. Decisions had to be made quickly, since the filing deadline for the next election was less than a week away.

Richards expressed concern over her recent separation from her husband and her previous treatment for alcohol dependency. Jane Hickie laughs and indicates that Richards's overriding concerns at the end of her thirty-three-year marriage were more practical: "I think that Ann thought that after they were divorced, she would live in a plain, hot, small apartment with a cat and knit."[5] Nevertheless, Richards's friends would hear nothing of such a retreat from the world. Mary Beth Rogers recalls that everyone knew that no woman had been elected to statewide office in Texas in fifty years, but Richards's friends yearned to prove "that a woman *could* get elected to a statewide office in Texas. Everybody was hoping that the decision would be made to push forward. The thinking was that Ann was ready and was versed enough in Austin politics to warrant a bid for the job. From the standpoint of talent, savvy, and political know-how, Ann was ready.

And Harding was in trouble. That presented the opening that Ann and her people were looking for."[6]

With the possibility of Harding's conviction looming, his political donations dried up. Knowing that Harding held approximately $300,000 cash in his campaign stockpile, John Rogers—Mary Beth's husband, a political consultant—challenged the Richards crew to raise $200,000 in cash and commitments over the weekend, which they did. The campaign had begun. A third candidate in the race, Waco state representative Lane Denton, traveled from town to town ahead of Richards and described her as "not only a drunk, but a mean one at that."[7] Denton alleged that Richards continued to drink and that she had a mental disorder. However, voters use their heads and their hearts when deciding how to cast their votes. Richards had confronted her problem head-on, and she had defeated it. She had been knocked down, but she had gotten back up. Moreover, in Texas, a gentleman does not speak that way about a lady, even in a political campaign. Once all the votes were counted, Richards had polled an impressive 466,000 votes, with Harding getting 362,000, and Denton realizing a mere 139,000. A fourth candidate, John Cutright, barely registered. The indicted Harding then withdrew from the runoff. Richards handily won the general election to become the first woman elected to a statewide office in Texas in fifty years. She had a personal campaign debt of $400,000.

Richards knew little about the role of the treasurer, but she learned quickly. She wanted to be the best treasurer that Texas had ever had. Years later, she spoke of the political bifurcation of candidate and officeholder, of how someone may be good at one role without being competent at the other: "'Campaigning and governing involve two entirely different sets of skills. I have always believed that as a candidate, it's very important not to run your own campaign. It's hard for me not to be in charge.' Then, responding to whether mean-spirited campaigns affected her, she replied: 'Oh yes, I'm much stronger now. Perhaps that's the beauty of the process. You have to be pretty tough.'"[8]

As state treasurer, she automated the agency, buying equipment to automate processes and speed deposits to interest-bearing accounts. These changes earned the state millions, which paid for the new equipment in just two weeks. Richards then looked to money-handling practices at other Texas agencies and sped up the delivery of the cash from each agency to the treasury. She discovered that there was no cash-flow analysis in the state and that Texans were losing money as a result. By speeding deposits and insisting that banks pay proper interest on state funds on deposit, Richards made more money in her eight years as treasurer than all the previous treasurers had made in their combined 146 years in office.[9]

Richards campaigned across the state and the nation for candidates and causes that she believed in. She became a favorite at political roasts. In 1988, at the Texas Democratic state convention in Houston, Richards was a featured speaker, and she generated excitement with her speech. Paul Kirk, who would soon become chairman of the national party, was present, heard the speech, and saw the reaction that it drew. As a result, he became convinced that Richards would become a national star in the Democratic Party.

The keynote speech at a national convention always goes to a governor or a national legislator of some prominence. Years earlier, Richards's friend Barbara Jordan of Texas gave the address. It was difficult to imagine at the time that a state treasurer would be considered for such an important role. Nonetheless, Kirk was convinced that Richards was the right person for the task. When members of the national press asked what she thought about being asked to give the keynote speech, Richards explained that she "had just that week completed 'major addresses' to the Madisonville Cattleman's Association in rural central Texas and the McAllen Mexican-American Democratic symposium in the Rio Grande Valley."[10] Jane Hickie had one overpowering concern about the speech: lighting! She called on Hollywood friend Lily Tomlin, who agreed to send the man who did her lighting. During the television coverage of most speeches at national conventions, "They'll let the speaker start, and then they turn around the national network cameras to the audience, showing people in weird hats and turning to people who are interviewing other people. They may or may not come back to the speaker, depending upon what they have to say and may go up to a broadcast booth, or whatever. So the deal made with the networks was that they had to take the house lights down for her keynote address."[11] The problem was that moments before Richards was due to begin her speech, Hickie realized that the house lights were still brightly lit, despite the deal. Hickie had to resolve this issue quickly. She is proud that she delivered an ultimatum: "'You bring those house lights down, or she won't talk!' So they did, and it was like putting a cloth on a birdcage; everybody just settled down."[12]

The crowd was electrified, and the performance was flawless. The British Broadcasting Company—the BBC—called and wanted to send a plane for her to come to London. Richards had connected with the nation and the world. Recalls Hickie, "It was Ann talking about the things that mattered to her. And the next morning, Ann watched the speech, and she said, 'I don't know who that old white-haired lady is, but she gave one hell of a talk!'"[13] Sitting in the audience was Attorney General Jim Mattox, who had his sights on the Texas governorship and who saw Richards as a threat to that goal. Mattox had tried unsuccessfully to get Richards removed from consideration for the keynote address. During her speech, he sat with arms folded and told people around him that in two weeks, no one would remember who had delivered that speech. When they did remember, Mattox unleashed a barrage of character assassinations against Richards the reformed alcoholic, telling a rally: "I just don't know if I can control my Baptist preacher friends any longer from attacking Ann about her drinking. I have many clients and many friends who have been on the wagon and then have fallen off. The statistics would show that a relapse occurs in a high percentage of cases."[14] Mattox went on to suggest that Richards used illegal drugs, even though the campaign had not yet even officially begun.

Political observers knew that the Democratic primary was shaping up to be a colorful, yet dirty, affair between two progressive candidates who once had been friends. Richards and her husband had worked as volunteers in previous Mattox campaigns.[15] However, something of a surprise was in store. Just before the filing date in December 1989, a third serious contender filed for the office: former governor Mark White. With Mattox and Richards bloodying each other in the more liberal wing of the party, the more conservative White and his team reasoned that if he could make the runoff and pick up some of the loser's votes, he would be the nominee.

The Richards campaign organization was prepared to take on Mattox and felt that Mattox had to be knocked down, while White had to be eliminated in the first primary. In Richards's commercials, a previous indictment of Mattox was mentioned, and, with a one-two punch, suggestions were made that White had improperly received financial benefit for his actions while in office. Hickie—who takes responsibility for the television spot—says that Richards regretted this tactic for the rest of her life. Hickie explains that Richards balked at the proposed strategy of linking Jim Mattox with Mark White and showing both in a bad light. Others also felt this approach might be too risky. Hickie says, "I said we ought to do it, and we did it. And I do feel responsible for it. I don't regret it a second. It caused us to win."[16]

Mark White remembers being targeted also by the attack on Mattox, to which White attributes his defeat. Before the attack ad ran, based on polls that showed a tight race, White believed that he would probably win:

> Ann Richards has one ad that she puts on during the last seven days before the election. The ad started off saying something about Mattox. Then, she says that I line my pockets with state dollars, that I bought a million-dollar house, and something else. Well, first of all, I came out of office owing more money than when I started in the governor's office. It was a little hard for me to understand how she came up with that number; but the cumulative impact of that is what she said about Mattox stuck on me because I'm the last one she mentions. That tape ran for about a week. I fell from thirty-three or thirty-four points in the polls to twenty in one week.[17]

Hickie explains that as damaging as the television ad was for White, it was even more unfair to Jim Mattox. The advertisement mentioned his indictment, but never mentioned his acquittal. Hickie explains, "I figured that everybody had their own speaking parts."[18] The attacks that came from both sides, however, were nasty. Throughout the campaign, Jim Mattox alleged that Richards used illicit drugs, going so far as to specify cocaine as her drug of choice. Then Mattox attacked on another front. Because Richards was a proponent of gay rights and had some people on her staff who were openly lesbian, more than a whisper campaign developed. Mattox reportedly told several of the press to ask Ann about being in a hot tub with Lily Tomlin. While the unfounded charges of lesbianism could not be discussed so openly, Mattox took great delight in piquing curiosity about Richards's possible drug use. In a televised statewide debate, Mattox looked directly at Richards and said: "Ann, you look awfully sober tonight. If you're not off the wagon after what you've been through the last couple of weeks, then you're cured. But Ann, both Mark and I have known you too long, and we can understand why you don't want to answer the question. The Republicans won't be as gentle, regardless of how much you think it'll hurt you to answer the drug question."[19] She never did. In the first primary, Richards accumulated 561,080 votes (39.5 percent), to Mattox's 521,094 (36.8 percent). Former governor Mark White was out of the running, with an anemic showing of only 274,551 votes. He refused to take Richards's phone call of condolence.

In the runoff campaign, Mattox continued to hammer at the drug-use issue. Paradoxically, he called for an end to the mudslinging, and both staffs met to organize the truce. Nonetheless, the next day, Mattox called a press conference and insisted that Richards take a lie-detector test to let the people know what drugs she took and where she got them. About the drug allegations, Mark White concluded: "People used it long enough that finally people just forgave her."[20] With the public tired of the nasty campaign, the runoff proved to be anticlimactic. In the twenty-eight-day campaign, Richards increased her lead, winning with nearly 60 percent of the vote—639,126 votes to 479,388 for Mattox. The headline in the *Dallas Times Herald* was "Richards Wins in Mudslide." Now the progressive female, divorced mother, and recovering alcoholic with high negative ratings—who was down twenty-seven points in the polls—would face a multimillionaire entrepreneur who had never before sought office, Clayton Williams.

At the beginning of the summer in 1990, few observers thought that Williams would have any problem defeating Richards. Her poor poll results and her high negative ratings contrasted sharply with the favorable perception that Williams had gained through a series of high-quality television ads. A *Houston Chronicle* poll had Williams ahead of Richards by 48 percent to 33 percent. The public generally regarded him as a successful businessman who had created twenty-six new companies and countless jobs for Texans. He was a rancher, an oil-man, a banker, and a telecommunications entrepreneur. He intended to spend twenty million dollars of his own on the race. He would be tough on crime. Drug offenders could spend their time "bustin' rocks." Despite these formidable strengths, he was remarkably gaffe-prone, and was increasingly seen as valuing women only in sexual terms. This was particularly problematic for someone facing a female opponent.

In March, in an effort to better get to know members of the press and to augment his Texas cowboy image, he held a press extrava-ganza at his West Texas ranch. There, he could rope and perform and demonstrate that he was more than "all hat and no cattle." However, rains prevented the planned program, and he was heard saying, "The weather is like rape. If it's inevitable, you might as well lie back and enjoy it." The Richards camp effectively was able get the public to recognize and understand the theme of these gaffes and question the humaneness and intelligence of her opponent.

As the campaign progressed, Williams spoke of going to Mexico as a young man to get "serviced." It became widely told that he had hired prostitutes to "service" workers at his ranch. He called Rich-ards an "honorary lesbian" because of her stance on gay-rights issues. Jane Hickie puts it this way: "Thank God for Clayton Williams! If it had not been for Clayton Williams, we would have never got elected. Ann gives the campaign an enormous amount of credit because the campaign kept the pressure up on Clayton Williams so that he would continue to make mistakes."[21]

As the campaign unfolded, Williams admitted that he had paid no income tax in 1986, while records showed he had given large contri-butions to Republican politicians during that year. He further admit-ted in a debate before the election that although he had already voted early, he did not know what Proposition One was.[22] To make matters worse, he explained that his wife, Modesta, had looked into it and told him how to vote. The final straw was his refusal, on live television, to shake Richards's extended hand while berating her and saying, "I'm here today to call you a liar." Texas voters saw that as no way to treat a lady. Republican campaign strategist Karl Rove analyzed the Williams

*Governor Ann Richards appointed boards and com-
missions that reflected the diversity of the state.*

campaign this way: "A lot of money hides a lot of structural problems. I do not believe he became repetitious. He had no additional
message by the fall. And the two times that they tried to establish a
message, they failed to do so, and lots of us said, 'After you've kept
him in a cocoon for a year, why let him out the last two weeks of the
campaign?'"[23]

Rove did not believe that the gender-based issue was the biggest
weakness in Williams's campaign, even though he conceded that the
issue was important:

More important, though, three things occurred in the last month
of the campaign. When Clayton Williams refused to shake

Richards' hand, he looked bitter, beat, and small. When he goes
on the television in the final week of the campaign and says, "I
don't know what that constitutional amendment on the ballot
was [it altered the governor's State agency appointment pow-
ers], Modesta told me how to vote on it." This looks stupid and
not managerial and not the tough guy, business guy in control.
That hurt him. And it also hurt him when he said, "I haven't paid
income tax."[24]

Another factor in Richards's favor was voter enthusiasm for her
candidacy that translated into a willingness to support it financially.
Williams's campaign was financed largely by Williams himself, rich
donors, and political action committees. Richards, on the other hand,
benefited from over 33,000 donors who each contributed a hundred
dollars or less. Few in the lobby were on her side. As Jane Hickie recalls, campaign operatives would ask wealthy women, "How much
did you pay for those shoes?" and request a like-dollar donation.[25]

Williams outspent Richards by six million dollars. Nonetheless,
Republican suburbanites supported Richards. Even conservative
Dallas County could not deliver a majority vote for Williams. Out of
3,892,746 votes cast, Richards's margin over Williams was fewer than
100,000 votes.

Richards now had approximately two months to prepare to govern. She was ready to get things moving. When asked about her views
on essential qualities in gubernatorial leadership, Richards said that
originally her view of leadership was that it was complicated: "You've
got to know exactly what your goals are, who are the people who can
do it, and you call up everybody, and you all sit at the table, and you
pass out assignments, and it's kind of like all the homework is as-
signed, and then you tell everybody to check back to make sure everybody did what they were supposed to do till you get there. That's what
I thought leadership was."[26] However, she came to a much simpler
view of leadership: "Leadership is knowing what you want and then
communicating it to the right people. When you achieve a position
of responsibility, people are very anxious to try to carry out what you
want to do. They endow you with power, whether you have it or not.
So I suppose I think that my own qualities are that I do know what I

want on any given subject. And I usually have a pretty good instinctive knowledge about how to get it."[27]

As Richards prepared for governing, Texas faced an estimated budget shortfall of approximately five billion dollars for the biennium. The campaign had been largely about drugs, but the issues facing Texas were being dictated, to a large degree, by court orders, including more spending for public schools, prison overcrowding, and serious issues with mental-health facilities. In addition, Texas's inefficient tax system needed a significant adjustment.

To set the course for the administration, Richards took a small group of people to South Padre Island. The group included Mary Beth Rogers, Jack Martin, Cathy Bonner, Jane Hickie, and Bill Cryer, among others. "We came up with the notion that we would develop a hundred-day plan," recalls Rogers. "We worked out what our goals were. Insurance reform, of course. We wanted to open up that appointments process and bring in people who had never been on state boards and commissions before. We set about identifying key appointments that we had to make in the beginning, what the issues would be before the legislature, and how we wanted to operate. Then we had daily meetings from then until the time Ann took office."[28]

In her first State of the State address, Richards spoke of the beginning of a "New Texas." She promised a progressive administration that would better serve citizens. An ombudsman would be based in the governor's office to serve as a troubleshooter and to cut through the red tape that caused Texans to "get bounced from one office to another until their eyes blur and their feet give out."[29] Longtime political observer Mike McKinney observes that Richards used gubernatorial power in a unique way when dealing with agency bureaucrats. She was the first to wield power effectively over state agencies:

Ann Richards could scare the pants off an agency director. She told me that the highway department had laid out a master plan for Waco to eliminate the traffic circle. Her aunt—her mother's sister—called her and told her, "We are all going to demonstrate at the traffic circle on Saturday, and it would mean so much if you could be here and participate in the demonstration against the traffic circle." Now, I'm going to quote her: "Aunt Bess, God bless! I'm the governor of Texas. I can't be parading around and demonstrating at the traffic circle. I can call the state highway engineer if it gets me out of having to come to Waco; that's what I'll do." And so I asked her if she called him, and she said, "Well, hell, yes. Look, you do whatever you feel like you have to do with your master plan, but my Aunt Bess is putting the heat on me to come up there and demonstrate to keep that traffic circle." She said, "I can do all that, or you can take another look at your plan, whichever you think would be easier for you." They threw the plan away.[30]

The implications extended beyond that single incident, according to McKinney, who argues that Richards changed the way things had always operated previously: "Dealing with agencies was pretty tough back in the days before Ann Richards. Ann Richards didn't always use comical tactics to get her way. She had a number of aides who were very forceful and pretty much explained to an agency director that they could expect hell."[31]

Richards also called for ethics reform and the creation of a Texas ethics commission to review and enforce ethics laws. She called for legislation to reform campaign-finance laws. She argued that the people appointed to state agencies by the governor should be trained in the work of the agencies and should specifically keep an eye out for duplication of services and waste. Further, Richards felt that appointees should be trained in ethics. The new governor named Barbara Jordan as ethics advisor to the governor's office. While the bill that passed had been weakened from its form in her original proposal, new ethical standards in public service and campaign finance did become law. The Texas Ethics Commission was created as an oversight and review board.

With regard to the environment, Richards believed that it was time that Texas closed the loopholes that allowed those who served as regulators to walk through the revolving door into a lucrative position in the industry they had regulated. The permit process, she felt, should be revamped because hazardous-waste facilities should be located farther from human population centers, and permits should be issued more sparingly for new hazardous-waste facilities. Further, she pushed for a coastal-management plan and insisted that the legislature do something about unsafe drinking water in border *colonias.*[32]

Because of her initiatives, rules were implemented to stop the revolving door at the environmental agencies. The legislature created the Texas Natural Resource Conservation Commission (TNRCC), which, by consolidating the Texas Water Commission and the Texas Air Control Board, would for the first time combine the regulatory programs for air, water, and waste. In addition, she signed into law an act that dealt with the state's ability to prevent and respond to coastal and marine oil spills. In short, she strengthened major environmental laws.

Richards had campaigned on the importance of insurance reform. In her address to legislators, she promised that she would do three things to bring about consumer-friendly insurance reform: "First, I

Even HM Queen Elizabeth II listened attentively when Bob Bullock spoke, 1991.

am calling on the holdover appointees of the State Board of Insurance to resign by February 15. Their resignations will give us the opportunity to initiate management changes and clean up the mess. Second, if the holdover appointees refuse to tender their resignations, we will then move to put the State Board into conservatorship. Under a conservatorship, the management of the State Board would be turned over to the State Conservatorship Board, which would exercise power to correct the management and fiscal failures of the agency."[33]

To be sure, this show of gubernatorial resolve was unusual. Consumer groups gave her high marks for passing the most comprehensive insurance-reform legislation in Texas history, which affected everything from rate making to a law making automobile insurance compulsory. The State Board of Insurance was renamed the Texas Department of Insurance, and the groundwork was laid to give the board's authority, by the following legislative session, to a commissioner of insurance appointed by the governor.

Of additional significance is the fact that she was able to sign a tax bill that was considerably smaller than the one that had been predicted, while taking the discussion of a personal income tax off the table. She increased the strength of the governor's office for the long term by consolidating and restructuring state agencies, giving her control of the Texas Department of Commerce, the Department of Housing and Community Affairs, and the Film and Arts Commission. Furthermore, for the first time, the governor would be appointing a commissioner of education, a new highway commission, and a director of all health and human services agencies. The lay of the land had been changed considerably for some time to come, and the executive office had been empowered.

Before the end of her first year in office, Richards had called for the passage of a state lottery, had caused it to be passed in the legislature, and had seen it pass in a subsequent statewide referendum by a two-to-one margin, with the expectation that the state's coffers would swell by an additional $700 million in the biennium. Richards dramatically eliminated her high negative poll ratings, ending her first year in office with a 61 percent favorable rating.

The themes remained similar throughout the rest of her administration, and the progress continued with the passage of antistalking legislation, a massive public-works project of prison construction, infrastructure to provide running water to the residents of the *colonias,* and immunizations for children. In addition, Richards pushed to improve public education by decentralizing it, passing a law that gives principals and teachers more ability to run schools their own way. Finally, twenty-four hours before a court order would have shut down Texas schools, Richards signed a new school-finance plan that reduced the spending disparity between rich and poor school districts. It was dubbed the "Robin Hood" scheme.

Richards also proved to be progressive on the business front. Upon learning that the only automobile-manufacturing plant in Texas might be closed, Richards charged Cathy Bonner, the executive director at the Department of Commerce, with coming up with a plan to save it. General Motors's plan to close a number of plants paired the Arlington, Texas, plant with a plant in Ypsilanti, Michigan. Each would need to make a case for its continued operation, but only one would be permitted to survive. As Bonner recalls, the plant in question produced a big car that police departments ordered for use as squad cars: "We said we'd buy them at the state because they'd run on natural gas. If you make them run on natural gas, we'll start trying to get local governments to buy them. We [Bonner and Richards] flew up to Detroit and met with the head of GM. We started putting together incentives, but the union in Ypsilanti dug their foot in the ground and said, 'We're not making any concessions.' Meanwhile, the Arlington plant got all its vendors to cut their rates and their costs, and we came out on the winning side."[34] John Fainter recalls Richards's thinking that the head of General Motors agreed to see her only under the "two-headed-cat system," suggesting that the executive was merely curious to see what Richards was like.[35]

Richards and Bonner also worked successfully to bring the headquarters of the Southwestern Bell Corporation (later known as SBC) from Missouri to Texas. At the time, Southwestern Bell was in a handful of states, Texas being the largest. Most of its customers were in Texas, yet Southwestern Bell was based in St. Louis. A Southwestern Bell senior vice president whom Bonner and Richards had known as a board member of the Foundation for Women's Resources told Bonner that if she worked it right, Southwestern Bell would consider relocating its headquarters to Texas. The catch: the deal had to be kept confidential, and Southwestern Bell desired a downtown location with over 100,000 contiguous square feet of building space. In fact, the project was kept so tightly under wraps that the mayor of San Antonio did not know what business would be relocating there until one hour before the announcement. Recalls Bonner, "We had this big press conference, and Whitacre got up and said, 'Well, throughout this process, the only two people who knew about this were Cathy Bonner and Ann Richards. This just goes to prove that two women can keep a secret.' And that was a big coup because you very rarely get a corporate-headquarters relocation."[36]

Jack Martin asserts that Richards loved the job-creation part of her position more than anything else that came with being the governor: "She believed passionately in economic development more than anything else. She thought that if she could be the champion of economic development, she would, because she loved it. She loved creating businesses and loved making deals. Ann would much prefer being in a room with powerful CEOs cutting a deal to standing on the courtroom steps attacking some institution."[37]

A governor, through appointing officials, can change the face of Texas government. Richards the campaigner had said that she would do just that. As governor, she did. In this regard, Richards started out with a bang. She promised that her appointees would reflect the demographic composition of Texas. Within the first year of her administration, she achieved that goal. Forty-eight percent of her first 650 appointments were female, 12 percent were black, and 25 percent were Hispanic. Speaking of the importance of appointments that reflected the state's diversity, Richards said: "The difference that these appointments make is that the dialogue changes when everyone is seated at the table. It is the right thing to do, and it is the smart thing to do."[38]

However, Richards's first, and showcase, appointee proved to be a disappointment to Richards personally and to her administration generally. Lena Guerrero, a former Richards campaign volunteer and an Austin state representative, was, in many ways, the face of the "New Texas." Smart, articulate, and personable, Guerrero was seen by many—particularly by Richards—as an up-and-coming Democratic Party star. Richards appointed Guerrero to fill the vacancy left on the

Texas Railroad Commission when John Sharp was elected comptroller. Paul Burka reports that the day the appointment was made, Sharp received a call from an angry oilman who demanded to know, "Who the hell is this Leonard Guerrero?" Sharp answered: "It's worse than you think; it's *Lena* Guerrero."[39]

However, by all accounts, the tightly knit oil and gas community grew to appreciate Guerrero as a quick study and a fair commissioner. As Jack Martin recalls, Ann saw a lot of herself in Lena: "Ann saw a young woman who was ambitious and who had overcome some hard knocks and had a real bright future. Ann thinks of Ann Richards as the early county commissioner, and here's Lena as a state rep. Lena also played Ann very well. Lena made sure that she always reminded Ann of that. In any exchange between Lena and Ann, Ann had Lena's best interest on her mind, and Lena had Lena's best interest on her mind. So the dynamic was sort of set."[40]

Martin and other insiders could see that with these interpersonal dynamics, Lena's future would be bright, but unlike Ann Richards, many of them suspected that this would not necessarily be beneficial for the governor: "Ann was going to let Lena be something. Ann was going to let Lena have her big break. So Lena got the Railroad Commission job, and I would say there was some consensus at the time that there was a risk there. Nobody had any idea why."[41]

Martin sees this episode as part of a larger issue, the heady feeling of coming into power and how that feeling can cloud judgment and leave the newly powerful person vulnerable: "There's a window of about three months, and you can go back and look at when they got into trouble, and it is when they've been given new power. Either they just won the election, or it's the transition, or it's inauguration, or they've just been reelected, or they've become a chairman or a Speaker. You go back and track it, and that's when they always get into trouble."[42]

In a college commencement address, Guerrero spoke nostalgically of her own college graduation. Political opponents broke the news and released the tape, along with evidence that the commissioner was not actually a college graduate at all. Paul Burka believes the event "killed Ann."[43] Jane Hickie is more specific: "I think it was heartbreaking. And I was furious. As it turned out, the weekend that all of that was happening—and I don't know if Lena ever owned up to it with Ann—Ann, Lena, and I were on a campaign trip for a congressman in El Paso, and if I could have thrown her out of the plane, I would have! I think Ann was just hurt. I don't know that Lena ever apologized."[44] Guerrero went on to lose the 1992 election for the post. Richards's showcase appointee had embarrassed the administration and let the governor down. Jack Martin believes that this, coupled with Richards's appointment of a replacement to a vacant United States Senate post, figured prominently in Richards's failed bid for reelection.

When President Clinton appointed Senator Lloyd Bentsen to be secretary of the treasury, an important vacancy was created that Richards would need to fill. Henry Cisneros, the popular mayor of San Antonio, was considered. He considered assuming the vacant seat, but turned it down. So did John Sharp and Jack Martin. Both Bill Hobby and his son Paul were briefly considered for the post. The names of two congressmen, Jim Chapman from East Texas and Mike Andrews from Houston were batted around. Barbara Jordan caused Chapman's name to be removed from consideration, and Richards could not muster enthusiasm for appointing Andrews. Meanwhile, Senator Bentsen was pushing for a quick decision, since he was ready to get on with his new job at Treasury. Hickie recalls one day Richards telling her, "'Well, you're not going to believe this; but the guy who has made the best presentation of anybody about why he ought to be the nominee is [former congressman] Bob Krueger.' Richards said that he was fantastic in his presentation, and she said that he thought he was right for the position and that he knew all the reasons why he was the right choice."[45] However, after Richards had made her decision, it was decided that Jack Martin and Secretary of State John Hannah would meet with Krueger to discuss the campaign. As Martin remembers: "Krueger was leaving the governor's office, and John Hannah and I were waiting. Before Krueger got there, Ann Richards called me on the telephone in her raucous, loud voice and said, 'This is the worst mistake I've made in my entire tenure as governor. This guy cannot win the Senate race! I don't know how I got into the position where this is the only choice I had! This is going to be a disaster.' That was the day she decided to pick him."[46]

Richards's instincts proved to be correct. After a five-month tenure as United States senator from Texas, Bob Krueger was defeated by a two-to-one margin by state treasurer Kay Bailey Hutchison. Krueger, a Shakespearean scholar, ran a silly political campaign with television ads of himself uncharacteristically on a motorcycle, saying: "*Hasta la vista,* baby!" The event proved to be a significant win for the Texas Republican Party and a big black eye for Richards and President Clinton. Jane Hickie remembers that the White House was not amused: "Do you remember the movie *Dave?* They sent the vice president to Burundi. They had to send him away. Which is why Krueger went to Burundi: the people in the White House saw the movie *Dave.* You think I'm kidding, but no, I'm not. I was at the Governor's Mansion when they called. There was an encyclopedia at the Mansion, and Ann said, 'See if you can find out where Burundi is.' We got the book, and oh, we were just dying laughing."[47]

Although Richards could by now point to a long list of legislative achievements and a stronger economy, it seemed to *Texas Monthly* editor Paul Burka that she was not enjoying the job as much as she once had. When he asked her about it, she responded: "If you mean, 'Am I sadder, but wiser?' the answer is *yes.*"[48] In the same interview, Richards went on to tell Burka, "I've always said that in politics, your enemies can't hurt you, but your friends will kill you."[49]

A recurring complaint about the Richards administration had to do with her staff. As Jack Martin puts it: "Ann had some people around her who had the best of intentions, but who had been given real power for the very first time in their lives, and they rationalized being bullies by saying, 'The other guys did it for years.' That's the dark side of the 'New Texas.' The pluses are that it opened the process up to a lot of people who had never had the opportunity before."[50]

Paul Burka followed up with Richards a year after she told him that she was "sadder, but wiser" and asked what she had meant. She responded: "I'm wiser because government is much harder to change than I thought. I'm sadder because politics is a lot meaner than I thought. It's a game of 'gotcha,' and it's played by everybody. 'Gotcha' if you try to do it right, and 'gotcha' if you do it wrong. 'Gotcha' because people want instant gratification, but that is simply not going to occur. We take too much sport in other people's discomfiture."[51] If some members of her staff were interested in paybacks and the promo-

Governor Ann Richards and her motorcycle, 1992.

tion of a purely philosophical partisan agenda, little evidence exists that Richards was driven by either. Jane Hickie states, "Ann has a bad memory for people who have done dreadful things to her."[52] As governor, she was driven by the practical and pragmatic in politics.

In assessing her term in office, *Austin American-Statesman* political writer Dave McNeely commented, "Richards put a distinctive face and personality on her office. Her sparkling smile and white bouffant hairdo are known nationwide. She has the best sense of humor and speaking ability of any Texas governor since the late John Connally— maybe even better."[53] Richards's strengths, however, extended well beyond her public-speaking ability and her public image to her stands on issues, including taxes. McNeely noted, "Perhaps, ironically, the woman decried by Republicans as just another tax-and-spend liberal actually has been rather tightfisted. She agreed with Lt. Gov. Bob Bullock and House Speaker Pete Laney to have a no-new-taxes budget in 1993, and she accomplished that."[54]

Richards's popularity apparently stemmed from her personality itself rather than the careful manipulation of public perceptions. McNeely commented, "She exudes a sense that she really cares about people—and she does. Her warm personality gets through, even to those who have only seen her on television. Of the Texas Poll respondents, sixty-nine percent said she'd be fun to have over for dinner, and sixty-three percent thought her the kind of person who would be a close and trusted friend."[55]

Ironically, in her farewell interview with the press corps, Richards said that if she had known that she was going to be a one-term governor, she would have "raised more hell."[56]

9

GEORGE W. BUSH

*Far better it is to dare mighty things, to win glorious tri-
umphs, even though checkered by failure, than to take rank
with those poor spirits who neither enjoy much nor suffer
much, because they live in the gray twilight that knows not
victory nor defeat.*

THEODORE ROOSEVELT, *"The Strenuous Life," speech to
the Hamilton Club, Chicago, April 10, 1899*

George W. Bush being sworn in as governor of Texas with First Lady Laura, 1995.

GEORGE BUSH had a different pedigree from that of other Texas governors. He was a descendant of the fourteenth president of the United States, Franklin Pierce, and a fourteenth cousin of Elizabeth II, the queen of the United Kingdom of Great Britain and Northern Ireland. One of his great-grandfathers, Samuel Bush, was a close personal advisor to President Herbert Hoover, while another of his great-grandfathers, George Herbert Walker, a cofounder of Brown Brothers Harriman (a privately owned bank), was one of twelve men who in a private meeting persuaded Governor Franklin Delano Roosevelt to run for the presidency. One of his grandfathers was a United States senator from Connecticut; the other grandfather was president of the McCall Publishing Company, which published *McCall's Magazine*. Bush's mother's ancestors settled in Maine in the 1600s. His father was president of the United States.

Despite never having successfully run for public office, George W. Bush challenged a popular governor with the best record in office since John Connally, and Bush won by a decisive margin. At first, few thought he could pull it off. Even his mother told him that he could not win. He responded by telling her that she had been reading the *Washington Post* for too long and suggested that she move back to Texas, start worrying about schools, shirk the Secret Service, and start paying taxes, and then see how she felt.[1]

Governor Richards was a charismatic campaigner and public speaker, and she had the ability to raise campaign funds from across the nation. Nevertheless, her campaign seemed stuck. Although a master at debates and public appearances, she would agree to but one debate, which thrilled the Bush camp. Despite some formidable advantages, Ann Richards found herself in a race that was to be too tight to call, and when the dust settled, the challenger had won by 8 percentage points.

Richards's friend Cathy Bonner offers this explanation: "We wasted four years not building the Democratic Party. The governor is always the titular head of the party, and with four years—and a lot of money—we should have had the strongest grassroots support for all Democratic candidates, but we didn't. Richards didn't spend the capital, the resources, or the time on building a party. To do it would have been a big, bloody fight with labor, and she didn't have the heart for it. She wasn't really interested."[2] Although it may be easy to understand Richards's motives for this lack of action, the party paid a high price for it. Bonner adds, "The result was at the end of four years, the Democratic Party had absolutely zip in credibility, resources, or organization."[3]

In addition to the things that Richards had not done to build a stronger political base, this time she would not be handed the office—as Clayton Williams had handed it to her. George W. Bush, Bonner notes, entered the arena with wind in his sails on account of his family name: "You put on that the name of *Bush* running. The person and the name, and it all came together. His willingness to take on the issues of what every poll said was what people were most concerned about and her unwillingness to do it. It just imploded upon itself. I think it is just something we have to live with that in four years, we let the party disintegrate. It wasn't just because of Richards, but it could have been stopped if it had been a priority."[4]

According to Paul Burka, the Republican advantage in the Richards-Bush contest can be explained in terms of population growth. In his article "George W. Bush and the New Political Landscape," Burka cites as an example the growth in Collin County. He explains, "Despite the lower percentage turnout, the county grew so fast that 26,000 more votes were cast; George W. Bush got 80 percent. Clayton Williams won the county by 13,000 votes in 1990; Bush won it by 31,000. Statewide, Richards actually received 90,000 more votes than she had in 1990, but Bush outperformed Claytie by more than half a million votes. Much of the growth in Texas has occurred in Republican areas of big cities and their suburbs. South Texas is growing too, but it lags behind the rest of the state in voter registration and participation."[5]

There are differences of opinion whether Richards's heart was in the campaign. Some say that she had grown weary of the job. Others insist that, because she was a political animal, her enthusiasm never waned. Bush's press secretary, Reggie Bashur, recalls discussing this situation with candidate Bush: "I don't think at the beginning of that campaign that he thought he was going to win. I think he thought it was going to be very tough to beat a very popular governor. But he wanted to try, and, I think in his mind, if he ran a good race and he came close—that would open a door for a future U.S. Senate race or something else. But as the campaign proceeded, '94 began to look like a big Republican year."[6]

Bashur indicates being puzzled by Richards's lack of drive for campaigning for reelection. Her opponent was also puzzled, but he was quick to realize the opportunity it presented: "Ann Richards, for reasons no one can understand today, did not run a very aggressive race for reelection. You know, if you go back, the records show that she made maybe one proposal the whole campaign—I think for teacher pay raises. She did not seem like she had the energy to run that race. This allowed Bush to become an accomplished campaigner. And on the plane, he said, 'She's supposed to be this celebrated campaigner—where is it? I don't see her campaign. I think she is giving us a real opportunity to win.'"[7]

Richards's friend Jane Hickie felt that while Richards did not want to lose the campaign, she did not really want to serve another term as governor. Apparently, she felt that she had an obligation to run even if her heart was not in the race. Robert Spellings—Richards's friend and the husband of Bush's U.S. secretary of education—recalls a conversation that he had with Richards as they sat in his car in the driveway of the Governor's Mansion discussing a second campaign: "Bush had not yet announced, but he was getting ready to. Ann says, 'You know, Robert, this boy could beat me.' And I said, 'Well, Ann, you don't have to run.' And she said, 'Oh, yeah, I've got to run. I owe too much to those people.'"[8]

Mary Beth Rogers agrees with the assessment that Richards felt obligated to run; beyond that, Rogers insists that Richards truly wanted to run: "I don't think that Ann enters into anything that she doesn't really want to do. She really wanted to do it. She also felt an obligation to run again. She felt like there were so many people that she had opened the door for—people serving on those commissions that had never come close to any position with that kind of authority before. That was new for Texas. Ann felt that she had an obligation to those people she put on the boards and commissions to follow through."[9]

Both Jane Hickie and Jack Martin conclude that Richards's enthu-

siasm for the day-to-day work of the governor's office had waned. Lieutenant Governor Bob Bullock made Richards's life difficult, almost
out of sport. On top of that, the daily attacks from Karen Hughes, the
Republican Party of Texas spokesperson, were relentless.

Jack Martin, John Fainter, and Mary Beth Rogers went to lunch at
the Governor's Mansion for the express purpose of saying to Richards,
"Your heart is not in this."[10] The governor reiterated the obligation she
felt to continue her campaign for reelection.

In what Mary Beth Rogers calls "the campaign from hell," Bush
stayed on script and was focused on just four issues: welfare, education, tort reform, and juvenile crime. The Richards campaign lacked
a unifying theme. Bush spoke of issues and his vision for Texas. Richards, speaking of Bush during the campaign, said, "This is not a job
where the federal government gives you job training funds so that you
can learn as you go. You can't be shaving one morning, look at yourself
in the mirror, and think, 'I'm so pretty, I'll run for governor.'"[11]

Bush stayed on theme; his utterances seldom varied from his
proposals. Perhaps learning from the tactics of Richards's previous
opponents—Mattox and Williams—Bush refused to criticize Richards personally and treated her in public with respect. However, in
a speech in Texarkana in August 1994, Richards said, "You just work
like a dog, do well, the test scores are up, the kids are looking better,
the dropout rate is down. And all of a sudden, you've got some jerk
who's running for public office telling everybody it's all a sham, and it
isn't real, and he doesn't give you credit for doing your job. So far as he
is concerned, everything in Texas is terrible."[12]

Although Bush chose not to attack Governor Richards personally,
others were more than willing to do so. Jack Martin looks back and
concludes, "We saw the beginnings of Ann's defeat in tactics similar
to those you see now in the Bush White House. We saw the attack
mechanism. Karen Hughes started it with her warm-up over at the
Republican Party of Texas, taking Ann on day in and day out. Karl
Rove's now well-known tendency to be able to create these wedge issues and turnout. Ann was the test case for all that."[13]

In the sole debate, Bush held his own against a masterful communicator. Consequently, the debate was generally viewed as a draw. In
the final days of the campaign, Dallas billionaire Ross Perot cut radio

spots endorsing Richards, but to little effect. The test case for spinning the campaign that Martin referred to was effective. Carefully crafted wedge issues created the perception that Richards's "New Texas" was not mainstream and that there must be something horribly wrong with it. Richards felt that she lost the race over guns, saying, "Bush was very firm on the concealed handgun legislation that he would sign it. I could not do it; in my conscience, I could not cross that line. He is governor because of guns."[14] In East Texas in particular, in addition to the gun issue, an underground campaign of rumors of lesbianism in the Richards camp began. According to Molly Ivins, the Richards staff created a joke game, in which "you had to put a bumper sticker on your car and drive through east Texas, and whoever made it back to Waco alive won. The bumper sticker was to say: 'I'M THE QUEER ANN SENT HERE TO TAKE YOUR GUN AWAY.'"[15]

In an effort to comfort her deflated campaign workers on election night, Richards said: "This is not the end of the world. It's just the end of a campaign." She was poised, self-assured, and probably somewhat excited about new challenges. Richards now wished to focus on making certain that her financial future was secure, so that, as she stated, she "wouldn't have to live out her old age in a trailer parked in one of her kids' driveways."[16]

Governor-elect George Bush hit the ground running. Before being sworn in, he met with all but two state senators and most of the leaders of the House of Representatives, generally charming them. He laid the groundwork for a solid relationship with House Speaker Pete Laney and Lieutenant Governor Bullock. Four years later, in Bush's reelection race against land commissioner Garry Mauro, Bullock would go against his political party and endorse Bush; Bullock had predicted that Bush would win. However, it was not only the party that Bullock bucked; Bullock was godfather to Mauro's daughter. Governor Bush could persuade others to join his cause.

Bush's success in doing so was particularly evident in the successes of his first legislative session. His highly focused legislative agenda had just his four main campaign themes: education reform, tort reform, tougher juvenile-justice approaches, and welfare reform. However, in 1995, in his first State of the State address to the legislature, Bush mentioned that he knew that the press had grown tired of hearing

Governor Bush and Dr. Seuss, 1998.

about the same four goals, so he laid out the fifth prong of his program. "Number five," he said, "is to pass the first four things."[17] As things turned out, he could claim victory on all five objectives.

Bush had great successes, but the job did not exactly consume him. Typically, he would arrive at the office by eight, but leave at 11:40 for a run and a workout, returning by 1:30 in the afternoon. Then, he would play video golf or computer solitaire uninterrupted until three in the afternoon.[18]

Because the Democratic Party controlled the House and Senate, Bush took a nonpartisan approach to campaigns. He refused to campaign against any incumbent legislator, since most of the powerful committee chairs and influential members were Democrats. He endeared himself to legislators and their staff members by popping into their legislative offices for casual chats. He had nicknames for many legislators. He attended the homecoming football game in Hale Center, Texas, with the Speaker of the House. When members of the legislature received favorable press mention, he often would underscore this recognition with a congratulatory phone call. In addition, Bush would have breakfast meetings at the Governor's Mansion with small groups of legislators. He watched legislative speeches on his office television and would congratulate legislators on particularly good performances. This personal attention accrued to his benefit. As Bush's secretary of state, Elton Bomer, remembers, "Bush paid a lot of attention to what you were adding to the process. He was interested in someone who could be progressive and add to the policy process, and he had a great habit of walking down the hall and having a good conversation with a member of the legislature about policy. He'd say, 'Here's why I'm interested in this bill, and I sure hope you can help me with it. I understand you have a problem with the bill, so what can I do to help you get past that problem?'"[19]

However, a governor, no matter how diplomatic or attentive to public relations, cannot satisfy the concerns of every constituency. While a gubernatorial veto pleases some, it simultaneously disenfranchises others. This would be the case with Bush's veto of the Patients' Protection Act. Many physicians across the state believed that insurance companies, particularly health maintenance organizations (HMOs), wielded a dictatorial upper hand and had too much influence over how doctors practiced medicine. Routinely, doctors charged, clerks at the end of a phone line in the offices of the insurance companies were making medical decisions. In addition, insurance companies were seeking to impose gag rules to prevent or restrict physicians from giving the best medical advice in some circumstances. The Texas Medical Association and virtually all members of the medical profession were vocal and up-front in their support of the legislation.

Despite this virtually unanimous support from within the medical profession, the legislation was flawed. Mandates, Bush believed, would actually increase the cost of medical care in Texas by some $500 million a year. In addition, powerful lobbyists had managed to insert language in the final bill that would have excluded from compliance two of the largest HMOs in the state, supposedly because their management structure made them different. To veto this bill would be to go against all the advice of those closest to the governor. One hundred eighty out of 181 legislators voted for the bill. As Bush recalls, "Vance McMahan, the policy director who knew that this bill would be used against me in a television commercial, was nonetheless sure we had to veto it. It was excessive government intrusion into the private health-care marketplace, he argued, exactly the sort of government overreach that an advocate of limited government must oppose. But my legislative director, Dan Shelley, was certain that I should sign it. Legislative directors generally encourage the signing of everything. They have to explain it to legislators if you don't."[20]

Governor Bush called in Elton Bomer, who was serving as insurance commissioner at the time, to make a presentation on the pros and cons of a veto. Bomer remembers making a presentation to Bush in his office, complete with flip charts, "as if I were still working at IBM Corporation. I said, 'Here is what the bill does, and here is what the bill doesn't do. I advise you not to veto the bill because the political implications will be dramatic.' He said, 'You let me deal with the political implications. I'm interested in your policy direction. Policy-wise, you think I'm making the right decision on this—you just think that it would be hurtful politically?' My answer was *yes*. He decided to veto the bill."[21]

However, the matter did not end there, according to Bomer. Bush was already thinking past the veto to his follow-up strategy, which proved successful. Bush won his long-term objectives, as well as winning support for his approach, despite the political cost that many had thought that the veto would entail. According to Bomer, "He said, 'Here's what I think we should do: I'm going to veto the bill. You let me know, as insurance commissioner, what power you have to enact the rules that will do everything in this bill that we can, with the exception of this one paragraph that I think is hurtful to health insurance and the State of Texas.'"[22]

After drafting a set of rules and proposing them as legislation, those rules "were enacted into law because the legislators liked the idea of rules. Within a week or two after he vetoed the bill, he agreed to meet with six or seven hundred doctors in Austin. He took me along to explain to the doctors why he vetoed a bill that they wanted so desperately. He told them what his plan was to fix the problem without passing the bill. So he became the hero of the health industry because he looked past the political implications to the policy implications."[23]

Terral Smith, Governor Bush's legislative director after Dan Shelley, believes that Bush's trait of decisiveness served him well. As an example, Smith explained how Governor Bush made veto decisions. Typically present in the room were Vance McMahan; Bush's advisor Karen Hughes; Albert Hawkins, who was in charge of the budget; Alberto Gonzales, chief counsel; and Smith. At times, Karl Rove was also present. According to Smith: "The governor would sit at the head of the table and listen to both sides of the veto argument. He'd ask questions, and let others weigh in. We would wait until we had about ten to consider, and then we'd call the governor and say, 'We need you to come and make some decisions.' He would listen to both sides. And Bush would say, 'I think I'm going to go with Terral on this; give me the bill.' Next bill, he'd say, 'Oh, I think I'm going to veto it. Next bill.'"[24]

Not everyone praised Bush's decisiveness, although Smith dismisses those objections. He notes that once, during a break, "Clay Johnson said, 'Doesn't it disturb you that he makes such a quick decision?' Karl Rove said, 'No. I worked for Clements, who had this reputation for being mean and tough. But he would go and bleed over these vetoes. He'd go home, he'd read it, he'd talk to outside friends, and he doesn't make any better decisions than Bush does. It is so much better to just go ahead and make your decision, good or bad.'"[25]

Elton Bomer underscores Smith's comments about the governor's decisiveness: "Bush made decisions very quickly. No one else I've ever been around in a close working relationship could make a decision as firmly and as quickly as he could after hearing both sides and asking a series of questions. And after we got through with the discussions, he would always go back around and ask, 'Is there anything else that hasn't been discussed here that we need to discuss?'"[26]

Once, however, Smith reports that the compassionate side of Bush played victor over the decisive side. Norma Chavez, a freshman Democratic representative from El Paso, had passed a bill that placed an insignificant regulation on certain businesses. McMahan argued that it was against the governor's philosophy to regulate industry unnecessarily and that the bill should be vetoed. Smith argued that the freshman representative worked hard on the bill and compromised with industry to the point that they signed off on its passage. Therefore,

Smith argued, the bill should be signed. Bush's decision was to veto the bill. Smith recalls what happened next:

> So, I called Norma to tell her the governor had vetoed her bill, and she started crying, bawling. Half an hour later, I went down to her office, and she was still sobbing. She couldn't even talk to me; tears were coming out. I said, "I'm sorry, I did what I could."
>
> So I went back to my desk, and at five o'clock, the governor comes by my office, and he asked, "Did you call Norma?"
>
> And I said, "Yes, I did. Governor, I think she is still crying! It meant a lot to her, and she's sobbing and just can't get over it."
>
> And he looked at me and said, "Let's get her bill back, and I'll sign it." So we went and pulled it from the secretary of state's office, and he signed the bill. After that, anytime he did a veto, Karl Rove would say, "Unless she cries!"[27]

Governor Bush prepared for the second legislative session with the knowledge that the state treasury would have a surplus of approximately three billion dollars. He also knew that a presidential run might be in the cards. Other Republican governors who might make the race had already cut taxes and spending in their states: John Engler of Michigan, Christine Todd Whitman of New Jersey, and William Weld of Massachusetts. Bush had yet to do the same. He proposed sweeping tax reform, including property-tax cuts. The large budget surplus gave him the opportunity to do so. As he recalls, "I decided to seize the money and freeze any plans to spend it by having a news conference to announce that the budget I would present to the Legislature would include a one-billion-dollar tax cut. I called it a 'billion-dollar-beginning.'"[28]

Bush failed to discuss his plans in advance with the presiding officers of the two houses of the legislature. Lieutenant Governor Bullock and Speaker Laney did not like to be caught off guard. They reasoned that property-tax reduction was a laudable goal, but questioned how the cuts would affect existing services. More questions, in their minds, deserved more answers.

Early one morning, while Speaker Laney was working on House committee assignments for his members, the phone rang. Lieutenant Governor Bullock was on the phone to discuss what he had just learned in the newspaper about the governor's tax-cutting plans. Neither appreciated the governor's surprise press announcement. Laney decided that the most thoughtful approach to the situation would be the surprise appointment of "a select committee of real tough people, chairmen of other committees. We would combine education and tax-revenue people who would not succumb to pressure from lobbyists—instead, the committee would be made up of people who understood Texas. Nobody on the committee knew that I was going to do it, except Sadler, and I told him about thirty minutes before I made the announcement. Several members of the committee did not like each other at all. And I did it knowing that."[29]

Bush reacted swiftly to Laney's announcement of the creation of a select committee to investigate, apparently realizing just as swiftly that both sides can use surprise as a tactic. According to Laney: "It wasn't but about a few hours after the committees were announced that I got a phone call from the governor, who said, 'I won't make that mistake again.' I said, 'What are you talking about?' Governor Bush replied, 'You know what I'm talking about—I'm talking about your committee. We need to visit about my program.' I said, 'That's a good idea, governor.'"[30]

The committee, in due course, rejected the Bush proposal and wrote a different one. In the end, there would be no major tax reform, but Bush could claim victory for property-tax reductions. After Bush assessed the situation, he concluded, "I'm glad I tried the major overhaul. I did learn some interesting lessons. First, it's hard to win votes for massive reform unless there is a crisis. If the courts had declared the school funding system unconstitutional, we would have been under the gun. With no consequences for inaction, action was difficult. The status quo is powerful, especially juxtaposed with fear of the unknown. Second, Texans appreciated bold leadership. I had earned political capital by spending it. All the dour predictions of damage for trying a bold reform were wrong."[31]

Bush had been bold privately and in public. He had employed a style that served his purposes. In a meeting with university chancellors who sought a billion-dollar appropriation for higher education, Bush asked, "'Would you accept five hundred million?' They immediately agreed. He then told them that he had been kidding about the five hundred million, but they'd acquiesced so quickly to a budget cut of fifty percent, they would have to come back to him with a justification why they needed the money at all."[32]

Because of the budget surplus, Governor Bush made tax cuts the cornerstone of his reelection bid against land commissioner Garry Mauro. He became the first Texas governor to be reelected to consecutive four-year terms, winning with approximately 69 percent of the vote. Almost two-thirds of all women voters, half of all Hispanic voters, a quarter of all African American voters, and three-quarters of all independents voted for Bush. He would go on to pass what would be, to date, the largest tax-cut bill in Texas history, which would include research and development tax credits, eliminate the tax on over-the-counter medications, raise the threshold for small businesses that must participate in the franchise tax, and create a once-a-year "sales tax holiday."

In addition, Bush would call for—and pass—measures to increase the number of charter schools and increase the homestead tax exemption. However, with a presidential run underway, the agenda lacked the boldness for which Bush was known. There are times, it seems, to play it safe. This was one such time.

The capitol was under constant surveillance from Japanese and European news crews. A former Canadian prime minister would be seen in the gallery of the Texas House. The Tory leader of the British Parliament would come calling on the governor. Boom cams from television stations lined the streets around the capitol. National television correspondents were as numerous as lobbyists in the halls of the capitol. Officially or not, the campaign had begun. In the legislative interim, Republican lawmakers spread out across the nation, campaigning in Iowa, Louisiana, or wherever their services were required.

When the victor was finally declared, Governor Bush decided to announce himself as president-elect from the floor of the Texas House of Representatives and to be introduced by his friend, the cotton-farming Speaker of the House from Hale Center, Pete Laney. As Laney recalls:

When I introduced Bush to the world that night, he and I were the only ones in the back hall by my office in the House chamber. And neither of us knew what we'd gotten ourselves into. But we knew the House chamber would be full. The only person in the back office with us was the CNN cameraman. And Bush says, "Now, Laney, don't go out there and mess it up because there are seventy-eight million people watching." I did not, as a country boy from Hale Center who was preparing to introduce the next president of the United States to the world, really need that pressure. I started to open the door, and then I shut it and turned to him and said, "Yeah, well half of them didn't vote for you."[33]

10

CONCLUSION

Democracy is a wonderful form of government—most of the time. But when you have to deal with 150 house members and 31 senators every time you want anything accomplished, you pay a price. Every new move, every reorganization, every appropriation brought a demand for something in return.

I fully understand a legislator's desire to bring a prize back to his district. There is a thin line between pork and bringing home the bacon; the legislators have to please their constituents to get reelected. But to accede to these demands more often than not is bad government. So much of your time is spent compromising, trying to persuade, trying to reason, trying to achieve your objectives without having a bill nibbled to death as it goes through the legislative meat grinder.

You witness the pride, the ego, the contempt, the greed, the selfishness of human beings to an unprecedented degree when you operate in a political environment such as state government. They practically hold you for ransom.

JOHN B. CONNALLY, *In History's Shadow*

GOVERNOR BUSH, as president-elect, told Lieutenant Governor Rick Perry that the governorship of Texas was the best job in the world. Months later, the new president of the United States called Governor Perry and asked, "Perry, do you remember what I told you about the governorship of Texas being the best job in the world?"

"Yes," replied the governor.

"Well, it's true!" said the leader of the free world.[1]

Indeed, those who have held the office tend to think highly of the experience. While serving, governors and their families live in a magnificent, mid-nineteenth-century Greek Revival mansion (the fourth-oldest governor's mansion in the nation). They can entertain legislators, supporters, and visiting dignitaries in one of the most historically significant residences in the nation. Overnight guests can sleep in Sam Houston's bed and pen a postcard telling friends about the experience while sitting at Stephen F. Austin's desk.

With a staff of approximately 150 people to work on policy and political matters, as well as to attend to personal concerns, a governor will have many needs and expectations covered without any second thought. The governor of Texas need not stand in lines. Pilots fly, drivers drive, personal chefs feed, and assistants fetch and deliver, while armed officers keep a constant vigil.

Typically, citizens are grateful when the governor of Texas cuts a ribbon to open a new public library in their town. Children are pleased when the governor recognizes their parents' fiftieth wedding anniversary by signing a resolution honoring the occasion. Graduates recall fondly that the governor delivered their commencement address. More than any other politician in the state, the governor can curry favor by doing favors.

As the personification of state government, a governor easily draws (and can generate) media attention. A former legislator decries that "the cacophony of legislator voices can rarely compete with a governor who can capitalize on the ability to command broad attention—which is surely one of the executive's principal strengths."[2] Staged events such as ceremonial bill signings and disaster proclamations ensure that a governor will receive credit for the ensuing good or relief (even though the governor may have had about as much to do with the bill's passage as with the occurrence of the disaster). Because a governor has no voting record, the disadvantaged can perceive the governor as sympathetic even if the governor never lifts a finger to address their concerns. Similarly, a skillful governor reads the movement of the legislature and gets out in front of its parade. The governor's ability to generate publicity can be a tremendously useful mechanism for advancing pet issues (since governors win their office—not mandates for their programs—with votes). To institute their programs, governors must persuade legislators, those who work in the news media, and members of the public.

Although the framers of the state constitution sought to limit— and succeeded in limiting—the influence of the governor's office, they overlooked one thing: power is a social game. Governors who are highly developed socially and who are driven to make changes can transcend the institutional limitations of the office. Paul Burka said of one governor that there were no benefits for being his friend and no consequences for being his enemy, yet this assertion is not true for every governor of Texas. Indeed, a strong governor creates those benefits and consequences and uses them to wield power effectively.

A collaborative governor who works with the legislature can realize numerous goals, often defying the naysayers, but an autocratic governor soon realizes the limitations of the power that he temporarily holds. As former Speaker Pete Laney says, "The power of the governor's office is dictated by how much the legislature wants to put up with."[3] To varying degrees, most governors of Texas have come to realize this. Clements realized this in his first term, while Smith learned this toward the end of his time in office. Most governors recover gracefully from the temporary illusion of self-importance that they may hold upon entering office. The smart ones realize: "The higher your station, the greater the need to remain attuned to the hearts and minds of those below you, creating a base of support to maintain you at the pinnacle. Without that base, your power will teeter, and at the slightest change of fortune, those below will gladly assist in your fall from grace."[4] Or as Mike McKinney, an aide to Governor Preston Smith, suggests, "There is a day when it all just slams shut, and all of a sudden, you can't get your phone calls returned. Just like that! I guess one of the things that I realize is that every governor who takes office thinks that he is in charge of the state. But when the legislature convenes, that feeling is rocked. That's when the governor realizes that he's not really in charge of the state."[5]

Any elective office in a democracy lacks absolute power. The actual power of an elected official is largely the effective or ineffective use of potential or inherent power. Every position of leadership comes with potential power that may be augmented or limited by realistically assessing opportunities and skillfully exploiting them. However, in the case of the governorship of Texas, in large part, the lack of absolute power is due to the status of the office by law, so that the powers of the governor remain limited unless other officeholders, particularly in the legislature, give express consent otherwise. Every schoolchild learns of the checks and balances of the federal government, but there are many checks and balances upon the power of the governor of Texas. McKinney explains that the state constitution in effect makes the legislature the ruler of the state: "The governor has some real power, but it is always in connection with a legislative body. It's always that the governor *may* do something with the consent of the legislative budget board or with the consent of the speaker or lieutenant governor."[6]

Power is a social game. The successful governor will understand people and their motivations. He will possess attractive personal characteristics, a measure of persistence, and a degree of courage and independence. Further, the effective state chief executive will have both a vision and a plan to make that vision a reality. The effective governor will motivate others to want that vision and plan to succeed.

However, in the power game of legislative politics, governors are surrounded by people who, for the most part, have no interest in helping them unless it is in their clear interest to do so. Constituents tend to understand a legislator's reasons for voting against a governor's agenda more readily than they will accept a legislator's explanation for supporting a plan that does not benefit them directly.

Over time, if a governor has nothing to offer a legislator's own self-interest, that governor risks eventually incurring the wrath of the lawmaker. Like the state senator who busted Connally's appointee "just to let the governor know I exist," legislators—as far as governors are concerned—know that "there is no more infuriating feeling than having their individuality ignored, their own psychology unacknowledged."[7] Governor Richards and Governor Bush understood the significance of the individual legislator, and both governors treated each legislator with appropriate respect—unless or until a legislator burned his or her bridges with the governor. Governors Connally and Clements, to varying degrees, paid a price for their lack of attention to individual legislators. Legislators saw both governors as aloof. The price in Connally's case was the Senate bust; in Clements's case, it was the first veto override in thirty-eight years.

The effective governor cannot afford to overlook a legislator's broken promises or misrepresentations. The effective governor balances the reward of being the legislator's friend and the loss of being his enemy. Jack Martin concludes, "If you ever get to the point where the majority of people you are dealing with think that they have nothing to lose by going up against you—you're gone!"[8] Paul Burka writes, "These axioms are especially important for a Texas governor, who occupies an office with little inherent strength and who therefore must earn whatever power he hopes to exercise. A governor has little authority over the executive branch, which is run by other elected officials in some instances and independent boards in others; he has even less authority over the budget, which is the province of the Legislature. A governor has only one power, really—the power to persuade."[9]

It is often claimed that Henry Kissinger, upon becoming secretary of state, mused that the thing he liked best about the job was that when he bored people, they thought that it must be their fault. Once the governor-elect has assumed office, his or her jokes suddenly become funnier. A common temptation is for governors to overestimate their own charm, which may lead them to make less effort to charm, seduce, or gently persuade their constituents and colleagues.

In addition to a governor's own political instincts, the most effective chief executives suffer people who are not afraid to tell them what they do not wish to hear. Staffers who can only answer yes permit governors to make errors that lead to bad leadership. One wonders whether a forceful staffer working in the governor's self-interest could have prodded Briscoe out of the do-nothing image that became so ingrained in the voters' minds. Could anything have persuaded Richards to roll up her sleeves to do the necessary party building? Her failure to do so eventually helped doom her reelection efforts. Similarly, one wonders whether good staff work might have prevented Dolph Briscoe's constitution flip-flop or White's confusing and divergent economic forecasts.

Good governors realize what is going on and discern whom they can trust. In addition, they give their former enemies reasons to trust them, realizing that allies are generally more useful than enemies. Effective governors know that in many cases an empowered former enemy often turns out to be more loyal than a friend, inasmuch as a former enemy will have more to prove. Ann Richards lamented that there is often more to fear from friends than from enemies. As she put it, "I've always said that in politics, your enemies can't hurt you, but your friends will kill you."[10]

Mark Twain said, "You can take a starving dog and feed him—and he will not bite you. This is the principal difference between a man and a dog." The effective governor, when asking for help, will appeal to a legislator's self-interest, but never to the legislator's mercy or gratitude. As Robert Greene and Joost Elffers write in their examination of power, in words that seem to echo Machiavelli, "If you need to turn to an ally for help, do not bother to remind him of your past assistance and good deeds. He will find a way to ignore you. Instead, uncover something in your request or in your alliance with him that will benefit him, and emphasize that all out of proportion. He will respond enthusiastically when he sees something to be gained for himself."[11] The politically astute governor, in short, will appeal to a legislator's self-interest. Governor Preston Smith effectively used this strategy when telling the University of Texas advocates that he was eager to sign their legislation—and would do so—once he first was able to sign the legislation for Texas Tech University, which caused them to have an interest in helping him with *his* goals.

In addition, a governor with a sense of humor—particularly a governor who can deftly deflect tough issues with humor—has an advantage over a humorless governor, no matter how earnest, hardworking, and dedicated to the public's well-being. Both Richards and Bush capitalized deftly upon their talent for humor, receiving media coverage outside Texas which they used to their political advantage. The high-

minded approach is not always best. Jane Hickie recalls a tense moment in the Richards campaign when the candidate was asked tough
questions about the death penalty: "A reporter asked, 'What is your
opinion on the death penalty?' Richards said, 'When I'm elected, I'm
going to uphold the laws of the State of Texas.' The reporter asked,
'Well, what would you do if the Texas legislature gave you a bill to abol-
ish the death penalty?' She said, 'I'd faint!'"[12]

In addition, effective governors are tireless activists for the causes
that they have proclaimed. This was the case with Governor Bush. As
Elton Bomer said of him, "When he made up his mind that something
was the right thing to do for the state, he would put all of his energy
and resources behind it, including his political capital, to accomplish
those things. So he got the reputation around the state that all you
have to do is listen, and you'll know what's likely to happen because
he's going to do what he says he's going to do."[13]

When asked, "What makes a good governor?" Reggie Bashur, the
press secretary to both Bill Clements and George Bush, says, "A clear
sense of purpose, knowing what you want to achieve. You need to go
into office with an agenda. Secondly, the ability to work with the legislature. It is an interactive process. The governor's office is only as
good as the level of cooperation that he can solicit from the lieutenant
governor, the speaker, and the members of the legislature. The governor must have that ability to interact in a constructive way. Third, a
governor must have people around who can do the same—cooperate,
communicate, and interact to move an agenda forward."[14] In addition,
Bashur went on to say that Bush—in particular—had no patience for
leaks. Bush demanded loyalty. Furthermore, he "had no patience for
staff or anybody else posturing. He wanted everything to be fair and
equal, on an open plane that was transparent, and for everybody to
work together and cooperate."[15]

Pike Powers, the chief of staff to Governor White, offers a different answer to the question of what makes a good governor: "Oh, I
think he, or she, has to be an effective communicator. I think they
need to understand that the legislative interests are very diverse, and
they need to be patient with that. They must be able to balance those
diverse interests and be able to communicate with the media. White's
great strength was that he'd walk into a room and within minutes he

would sense the pulse of the room to know what was happening and how to respond to it. He just had a very significant intuitive sense."[16]

Former state senator Babe Schwartz believes that a good governor has "courage, vision, the ability to articulate a vision, and independence. I tell you, I guess money is responsible for this, but show me a guy today who will do something on his own when his chief political supporters happen to be on that issue on the other side. They don't have any courage if they don't!"[17]

Former lieutenant governor Bill Hobby believes that for a governor to be good, he first must be a good person. Accordingly, Hobby concludes that Briscoe, of the governors he served with, was "the best person, the most humane, the most understanding, and the most compassionate. Bill Clements was the worst."[18]

Former Speaker Gib Lewis has a different take. He believes that a good governor, above all, must be open-minded: "The worst thing that I have found over the years is for the governor to have a tendency to want to showboat. If they can refrain from doing that, they make a lot better governor. But when you—and I've seen them all do it to a degree—get out and sign some highway bill in the middle of a Houston freeway at five o'clock in the afternoon—or some crazy deal like that—to showboat it—that turns people off. I think it works against them."[19]

Jack Martin believes that both Ann Richards and Bill Clements were good governors because they inspired hope in people for positive change. Ann Richards, Martin says, was a good governor "first and foremost because Ann gave people the hope that here was going to be something other than the status quo, and that it was something that they could get excited about, and they could really have their lives improved by it. That's not a philosophical or a party thing. I think to some extent, Clements did that when he got elected governor. I think Clements gave people the hope that the status quo wasn't going to be the same."[20] Other reasons for their being good governors, in Martin's opinion, came down to their character and personality traits: Clements's candor and Richards's pragmatism: "Clements had this refreshing candor, so it's not a partisan thing. What was wonderful about Ann was that she was a pragmatist. Ann could wheel and deal with anybody, Republican or Democrat. If you were willing to get in the room with her and be objective about Ann and what Ann stood for, then she'd trade with you all day long. But if you were one of these people who decided that she was evil before the meeting began, which a lot of people did, there'd be no chance."[21]

However, no matter how much the officeholder may seem larger than life, the office is bigger than its holder. Mark White found that out. He had skills as sound as those of anyone else who had ever served in the office, but the times were against his success. The economy plummeted. The things beyond the control of the chief executive—whether good or bad—present the biggest challenges to any governor. As Greene and Elffers conclude, "Luck and circumstance always play a role in power. This is inevitable and actually makes the game more interesting. But, despite what you may think, good luck is always more dangerous than bad luck. Bad luck teaches valuable lessons about patience, timing, and the need to be prepared for the worst; good luck deludes you into the opposite lesson, making you think your brilliance will carry you through. Your fortune will inevitably turn, and when it does, you will be completely unprepared."[22]

White began his first legislative session not only by declaring that the budget was sound, but also by further advising legislators not to let anyone tell them otherwise. Two years later, the state was in a financial crisis, with the value of oil having plummeted by almost two-thirds. Knowing how to assume office in good times—and not bad times—makes a good governor good.

Because governance in Texas is designed to be carried out by several independently elected persons, an effective governor is ever aware of rivalries that the governor can create or work to prevent. Sometimes it is important to have and to make enemies. Often, however, it is not. Governor Clements made an enemy of his attorney general, Mark White. Governor Briscoe underestimated the ambition of Attorney General John Hill. Both governors ended up being challenged by their rivals. To be sure, the plurality of the executive branch can create rivalries, and those rivals can sometimes overtake the leadership of the governor. To a lesser degree, those rivalries can make the life of the governor difficult, as in the case of Lieutenant Governor Bullock and Governor Richards, whose personal differences created scars that never healed cleanly.

Notwithstanding all this, perhaps the most important characteristics of a good governor are a thick skin and personal vision. It has been said that legislative politics can be vicious because the stakes are so low. Every governor examined herein has been tough, relatively immune to criticism, and focused on doing work that is bigger than his or her own personal agendas. A good governor is interested in the welfare of the next generation. Each governor, to varying degrees, has taken this approach. Long may this approach continue in the State of Texas and its highest elective office.

NOTES

Chapter 1

1. Burka, "Strange Case," 134.
2. Nixon, *Leaders: Profiles and Reminiscences*, 330.
3. Burka, "Truth," 285.
4. Rogers, personal interview, July 3, 2006.
5. Ibid.
6. Ibid.
7. White, personal interview, July 25, 2006.
8. Gantt, Dawson, and Hagard, *Governing Texas*, 197.
9. Gantt, *Chief Executive in Texas*, 89.
10. Article 4, Section 7.
11. Helprin, "Statesmanship and Its Betrayal," n.p.
12. Neustadt, *Presidential Power*, 203.

Chapter 2

The epigraph to this chapter is taken from Beschloss, *Presidential Courage*, 278.

1. Burka, "More than Myth," n.p.
2. Ann Richards and George W. Bush later held this distinction.
3. Banks, *Money, Marbles, and Chalk*, 159.
4. Read, personal interview, June 20, 2006.
5. Ibid.
6. Davis, personal interview, Apr. 26, 2006.
7. Crawford and Keever, *John B. Connally*, 90.
8. Connally, address, Fifty-eighth Legislature, 68.
9. Ibid., 69.
10. Ibid.
11. Temple, personal interview, May 1, 2006.
12. Read, personal interview.
13. Stromberger was also later the capital correspondent for the *Dallas Times Herald*.
14. Stromberger, personal interview, May 2, 2006.

15. Crawford and Keever, *John B. Connally,* 99.

16. Connally, address, Fifty-eighth Legislature, 67.

17. Crawford and Keever, *John B. Connally,* 96.

18. Quoted in Pittman, *Inside the Third House,* 35.

19. Krajl, personal interview, July 5, 2006.

20. Schwartz, personal interview, June 13, 2006.

21. Mobley, personal interview, May 2, 2006.

22. Crawford and Keever, *John B. Connally,* 102.

23. Quoted in Barnes, *Barn Burning, Barn Building,* 79.

24. Connally, address, Fifty-ninth Legislature, 74.

25. Crawford and Keever, *John B. Connally,* 128.

26. Burka, "More than Myth," n.p.

Chapter 3

The epigraph to this chapter is by John Henry Faulk, quoted in Kinch and Proctor, *Texas under a Cloud,* 37.

1. Crawford and Keever, *John B. Connally,* 112.

2. Ibid., 125.

3. Conn, *Preston Smith,* 79.

4. Ibid., 73.

5. Crawford and Keever, *John B. Connally,* 125.

6. Ibid.

7. Quoted in Conn, *Preston Smith,* 122.

8. McLendon had dropped out of the race in February.

9. Barnes, *Barn Burning, Barn Building,* 166.

10. Smith, State of the State address, 111.

11. Ibid., 117.

12. Stromberger, personal interview.

13. Ibid.

14. Delwin Jones, personal interview, May 3, 2006.

15. Banks, *Money, Marbles, and Chalk,* 50.

16. McKinney, personal interview, Apr. 25, 2006.

17. Ibid.

18. Ibid.

19. Banks, *Money, Marbles, and Chalk,* 41.

20. McKinney, personal interview.

21. Stromberger, personal interview.

22. Preston Smith, address, Sixty-second Legislature, 95.

23. Pittman, *Inside the Third House,* 46.

24. Stromberger, personal interview.

25. McKinney, personal interview.
26. Ibid.

Chapter 4
1. Briscoe, address, Sixty-sixth Legislature, 1.
2. Banks, *Money, Marble, and Chalk*, 30.
3. Barnes, *Barn Burning, Barn Building*, 190.
4. Schwartz, personal interview.
5. Hobby, personal interview, July 25, 2006.
6. Nixon Presidential Library, *Tape 813 Conversations*.
7. Ibid.
8. Quoted in Barnes, *Barn Burning, Barn Building*, 216.
9. Nixon Presidential Library, *Tape 813 Conversations*.
10. Ibid.
11. White, personal interview.
12. Ibid.
13. Hobby, personal interview.
14. Briscoe, address, Sixty-third Legislature, 136.
15. Ibid., 142.
16. Montgomery, "Briscoe So-So in His First Crucial Test."
17. Montgomery, "Texas First Lady."
18. Porterfield, "Gov. Briscoe Has Everything."
19. Lee Jones, "Charting the Governor's Elusive Path."
20. *Dallas Times Herald,* "Erwin Calls Briscoe's Office Weak."
21. Montgomery, "Briscoe Appears Unbeatable."
22. Briscoe, address, Sixty-third Legislature, 137.
23. *Dallas Times Herald,* "Bullock Calls Hill 'S.O.B.'"

Chapter 5
The epigraph to this chapter is from Faulk, *Uncensored John Henry Faulk,* 18.
1. Francis, personal interview, June 26, 2006.
2. Burka, "Governor's New Clothes," 128.
3. Ibid.
4. Barta, *Bill Clements,* 33.
5. Ibid., 129.
6. Ibid., 197.
7. Burka, "Governor's New Clothes," 129.
8. Francis, personal interview.
9. George H. W. Bush had hired Rove in 1977.
10. Toomey, personal interview, Apr. 20, 2006.

11. Francis, personal interview.
12. Barta, *Bill Clements*, 211.
13. Laney, personal interview, Apr. 26, 2006.
14. Barta, *Bill Clements*, 228.
15. Kuempel, "Governor Stands Firm."
16. Laney, personal interview.
17. Kinch, "Clements Gets Silence Treatment."
18. Hobby, personal interview.
19. Ibid.
20. Barta, *Bill Clements*, 225.
21. Attlesey, "Clements Heaves Sigh."
22. Francis, personal interview.
23. Ibid.
24. Barta, *Bill Clements*, 261.
25. Democratic state senator Bill Braecklein initially resisted changing par-
    ties, but then he switched parties to run for reelection as a Republican.
    However, by that time, John Leedom, who had been a member of the
    Republican Party for a long time, won handily.
26. Phil Gramm resigned from Congress and ran for a senate seat, which he
    won.
27. Francis, personal interview.
28. Dean had been secretary of state under Briscoe.
29. Clements, "To James Michener," June 8, 1981; quoted in Barta, *Bill Cle-
    ments*, 259.

Chapter 6

The epigraph to this chapter is taken from Ivins and Dubose, *Shrub*, 130–131.
 1. White, personal interview.
 2. Burka, "Mark White's Coming Out Party," 145.
 3. Barta, *Bill Clements*, 232.
 4. Ibid., 259.
 5. White, personal interview.
 6. Barta, *Bill Clements*, 240.
 7. Quoted in ibid.
 8. Bashur, personal interview, Apr. 21, 2006.
 9. White, personal interview.
10. Barta, *Bill Clements*, 274.
11. Ibid., 275.
12. Rodrique, "Clements Plays for High Stakes," 100.
13. This was a veiled reference to President Kennedy's youngest brother,

Senator Edward Kennedy, and the scandal surrounding his presence at the drowning death of Mary Jo Kopechne at Chappaquiddick and his delay in notifying the police of the fatal car accident.

14. Barta, *Bill Clements*, 275.
15. Quoted in ibid., 287. The story was reported in the *Dallas Morning News*, November 7, 1982.
16. Powers, personal interview, Apr. 21, 2006.
17. White, personal interview.
18. Barta, *Bill Clements*, 288.
19. Kuempel, "Appointments Battle."
20. Powers, personal interview.
21. Ibid.
22. White, personal interview.
23. Kuempel, "Appointments Battle."
24. White, address, Sixty-eighth Legislature, 191.
25. *Dallas Times Herald*, "Sixty-Eighth Legislature."
26. White, address, Sixty-ninth Legislature, 115.
27. White, personal interview.
28. Ibid.
29. Ibid.
30. The Permanent University Fund originated in 1839 when the Congress of the Republic of Texas set aside fifty leagues (221,400 acres) of land to fund higher education in Texas. None of the principal of the fund can be spent. The fund's proceeds derive from oil, gas, sulfur, and water royalties; gains on investments; rentals on mineral leases; and sales of land. The public endowment provides support for the University of Texas and the Texas A&M University systems (Smyrl, "Permanent University Fund").
31. Powers, personal interview.
32. Burka, "Strange Case of Mark White," 212.
33. McNeely, "Subdued Legislature Regarded as Efficient."
34. White, legislative accomplishments press conference. Microelectronics and Computer Technology Corporation (MCC) was a highly sought-after computer-research consortium.
35. White, personal interview.
36. Ibid.
37. White, address, Sixty-ninth Legislature, 115.
38. Anthony, "White Draws Low Marks."
39. Burka, "Strange Case of Mark White," 134. In these comments, the un-named former governor was Bill Clements.

Chapter 7

1. Barta, *Bill Clements*, 318.
2. White, personal interview.
3. Ibid.
4. Ibid.
5. Ibid.
6. Powers, personal interview.
7. Ibid.
8. Bashur, personal interview.
9. Ibid.
10. Ibid.
11. Ibid.
12. Ibid.
13. Barta, *Bill Clements*, 349.
14. Ramsey, "Clements: He's Ready to Leave."
15. Camuto, "Clements Shifts Gears."
16. Barta, *Bill Clements*, 367.
17. Ramsey, "Clements: He's Ready to Leave."

Chapter 8

The epigraph to this chapter is taken from Connally and Herskowitz, *In History's Shadow*, 360–361.

1. Richards, *Straight from the Heart*, 13.
2. The only woman who had served as governor before Richards was Miriam Ferguson, who was elected governor after her husband, Governor Jim Ferguson, was impeached. She ran on the slogan "Two governors for the price of one," so it would be tough to argue that she was elected in her own right rather than riding into office on her husband's coattails.
3. Shropshire and Schaefer, *Thorny Rose of Texas*, 122.
4. Hickie, personal interview, July 29, 2006.
5. Ibid.
6. Shropshire and Schaefer, *Thorny Rose of Texas*, 150.
7. Ibid., 161.
8. Burka, "Ann of a Hundred Days," 128.
9. Richards, *Straight from the Heart*, 232.
10. Shropshire and Schaefer, *Thorny Rose of Texas*, 175.
11. Hickie, personal interview.
12. Ibid.
13. Ibid.
14. Shropshire and Schaefer, *Thorny Rose of Texas*, 186.

15. David Richards had been an assistant attorney general under Mattox.
16. Hickie, personal interview.
17. White, personal interview.
18. Hickie, personal interview.
19. Shropshire and Schaefer, *Thorny Rose of Texas*, 193.
20. White, personal interview.
21. Hickie, personal interview.
22. It was the only constitutional amendment proposition on the ballot, and it concerned gubernatorial power.
23. Tolleson-Rinehart, *Claytie and the Lady*, 91.
24. Ibid. The millionaire had used the tax code in 1986 to avoid paying any income tax.
25. Hickie, personal interview.
26. Tolleson-Rinehart, *Claytie and the Lady*, 139.
27. Ibid.
28. Rogers, personal interview.
29. Richards, State of the State address, 1991.
30. McKinney, personal interview.
31. Ibid.
32. *Colonias* are communities on the Texas side of the border with Mexico. They often lack running water or sewer service, and are marked by widespread poverty and substandard living conditions.
33. Richards, State of the State address, 1991.
34. Bonner, personal interview, May 3, 2006.
35. John Fainter, personal interview, Apr. 26, 2006.
36. Ibid. Edward Whitacre was the chairman of Southwestern Bell.
37. Martin, personal interview, July 28, 2006.
38. Tolleson-Rinehart, *Claytie and the Lady*, 143.
39. Burka, "Ann of a Hundred Days," 129.
40. Martin, personal interview.
41. Ibid.
42. Ibid.
43. Burka, personal interview, May 2, 2006.
44. Hickie, personal interview.
45. Ibid.
46. Martin, personal interview.
47. Hickie, personal interview.
48. Burka, "Sadder but Wiser," 90.
49. Ibid., 140.
50. Martin, personal interview.

51. Burka, "Sadder but Wiser," 92.
52. Hickie, personal interview.
53. Quoted in Shropshire and Schaefer, *Thorny Rose of Texas*, 234.
54. Ibid.
55. Ibid.
56. Ivins, *Who Let the Dogs In?* 175.

Chapter 9

1. Mitchell, *W: The Revenge*, 296.
2. Bonner, personal interview.
3. Ibid.
4. Ibid.
5. Burka, "George W. Bush."
6. Bashur, personal interview.
7. Ibid.
8. Spellings, personal interview, July 10, 2006.
9. Rogers, personal interview.
10. Martin, personal interview.
11. Bush, *A Charge to Keep*, 33.
12. Ibid.
13. Martin, personal interview.
14. Ivins and Dubose, *Shrub*, 44.
15. Ibid., 45.
16. Bonner, *What I Want Next*, 26.
17. Bush, State of the State address (1995), 6.
18. Mitchell, *W: The Revenge*, 325.
19. Bomer, personal interview, Apr. 20, 2006.
20. Bush, *A Charge to Keep*, 193.
21. Bomer, personal interview.
22. Ibid.
23. Ibid.
24. Terral Smith, personal interview.
25. Ibid.
26. Bomer, personal interview.
27. Terral Smith, personal interview.
28. Bush, *A Charge to Keep*, 123–124.
29. Laney, personal interview. Paul Sadler was the chair of the committee.
30. Ibid.
31. Bush, *A Charge to Keep*, 129–130.

32. Mitchell, *W: The Revenge,* 325.
33. Laney, personal interview.

Chapter 10

The epigraph to this chapter is taken from Connally and Herskowitz, *In History's Shadow,* 227–228.

1. Perry, personal interview, July 6, 2006.
2. Rosenthal, *Governors and Legislatures' Contending Powers,* 25.
3. Laney, personal interview.
4. Greene and Elffers, *48 Laws of Power,* 370.
5. McKinney, personal interview.
6. Ibid.
7. Greene and Elffers, *48 Laws of Power,* 372.
8. Martin, personal interview.
9. Burka, "Strange Case of Mark White," 136.
10. Burka, "Sadder but Wiser," 59.
11. Greene and Elffers, *48 Laws of Power,* 95.
12. Hickie, personal interview.
13. Bomer, personal interview.
14. Bashur, personal interview.
15. Ibid.
16. Powers, personal interview.
17. Schwartz, personal interview.
18. Hobby, personal interview.
19. Lewis, personal interview, July 28, 2006.
20. Martin, personal interview.
21. Ibid.
22. Greene and Elffers, *48 Laws of Power,* 415.

BIBLIOGRAPHY

Anthony, Linda. "White Draws Low Marks for Work with Legislature." *Austin American-Statesman*. Austin: Texas State Archives, n.d.

Attlesey, Sam. "Clements Heaves Sigh Over Session." *Dallas Morning News,* May 11, 1979.

Banks, Jimmy. *Money, Marbles, and Chalk.* Austin: Texas Publishing, 1972.

Barnes, Ben, with Lisa Dickey. *Barn Burning, Barn Building: Tales of a Political Life from LBJ through George W. Bush and Beyond.* Albany, Tex.: Bright Sky Press, 2006.

Barta, Carolyn. *Bill Clements: Texian to his Toenails.* Austin: Eakin Press, 1996.

Bashur, Reggie. Personal interview. Apr. 21, 2006.

Beschloss, Michael. *Presidential Courage: Brave Leaders and How They Changed America, 1789–1989.* New York: Simon & Schuster, 2007.

Beyle, Thad, ed. *Governors and Hard Times.* Washington, D.C.: CQ Press, 1992.

Bomer, Elton. Personal interview. Apr. 20, 2006.

Bonner, Cathy. Personal interview. May 3, 2006.

———. *What I Want Next.* Austin, Tex.: Sag Harbor Press, 2006.

Briscoe, Dolph. Address. Sixty-third Legislature of the State of Texas. *Journal of the House of Representatives,* Jan. 9, 1973.

———. Address. Sixty-fourth Legislature of the State of Texas. *Journal of the House of Representatives,* Jan. 14, 1975.

———. Address. Sixty-fifth Legislature of the State of Texas. *Journal of the House of Representatives,* Jan. 11, 1977.

———. Address. Sixty-sixth Legislature of the State of Texas. *Journal of the House of Representatives,* Jan. 16, 1979.

———. First Inaugural Address, Jan. 16, 1973.

———. *Official State Papers.* Austin: Center for American History at the Univ. of Texas at Austin.

———. Second Inaugural Address, Jan. 21, 1975.

Bullock, Bob. Letter. Mar. 23, 1987. Waco, Tex.: Bullock Archives, Baylor University.

Burka, Paul. "Ann of a Hundred Days." *Texas Monthly,* May 1991, 126–128, 130, 132, 134.

———. "George W. Bush and the New Political Landscape: How the Republicans Beat Ann Richards and Took Over Texas." *Texas Monthly,* Dec. 1994.

———. "The Governor's New Clothes." In *Texas Monthly's Political Reader,* 125–131. 3rd ed. Austin: Texas Monthly Press, 1985.

———. "Mark White's Coming Out Party." In *Texas Monthly's Political Reader,* 144–147. 3rd ed.

———. "More than Myth." *Texas Monthly,* Aug. 1993. http://www.ebscohost .com/. (accessed May 3, 2006).

———. Personal interview. May 2, 2006.

———. "Sadder but Wiser." *Texas Monthly,* Apr. 1995, 59–61, 90–92, 139–140.

———. "The Strange Case of Mark White." *Texas Monthly,* Oct. 1986, 134–135.

———. "The Truth about John Connally." *Texas Monthly,* Nov. 1979, 157–161, 267–268, 270, 272, 275, 276, 278, 280, 282, 284–287.

Bush, George W. Address. Seventy-fifth Legislature of the State of Texas. *Journal of the House of Representatives,* Jan. 14, 1997.

———. *A Charge to Keep.* New York: Morrow, 1999.

———. First Inaugural Address, Jan. 17, 1995.

———. Second Inaugural Address, Jan. 19, 1999.

———. State of the State Address, Feb. 7, 1995.

———. State of the State Address, Jan. 27, 1999.

Camuto, Robert V. "Clements Shifts Gears in Style of Governing." *Dallas Times Herald,* Jan. 29, 1989.

Clements, William P., Jr. Address. Sixty-sixth Legislature of the State of Texas. *Journal of the House of Representatives,* Jan. 9, 1979.

———. Address. Sixty-seventh Legislature of the State of Texas. *Journal of the House of Representatives,* Jan. 13, 1981.

———. Address. Seventieth Legislature of the State of Texas. *Journal of the House of Representatives,* Jan. 13, 1987.

———. Address. Seventy-first Legislature of the State of Texas. *Journal of the House of Representatives,* Jan. 10, 1989.

———. First Inaugural Address, Jan. 16, 1979.

———. "To James Michener," June 8, 1981. Quoted in Barta, 259.

———. *Official State Papers.* College Station: Texas A&M Univ.; Austin: Texas State Archives.

———. Second Inaugural Address, Jan. 20, 1987.

Conn, Jerry Douglas. *Preston Smith: The Making of a Texas Governor.* Austin, Tex.: Jenkins, 1972.

Connally, John B. Address. Fifty-eighth Legislature of the State of Texas. *Journal of the House of Representatives,* Jan. 8, 1963.

———. Address. Fifty-ninth Legislature of the State of Texas. *Journal of the House of Representatives,* Jan. 12, 1965.

———. Address. Sixtieth Legislature of the State of Texas. *Journal of the House of Representatives,* Jan. 10, 1967.

———. First Inaugural Address, Jan. 15, 1963.

———. Second Inaugural Address, Jan. 26, 1965.

———. Third Inaugural Address, Jan. 17, 1967.

Connally, John, and Mickey Herskowitz. *In History's Shadow: An American Odyssey.* New York: Hyperion, 1993.

Crawford, Ann Fears, and Jack Keever. *John B. Connally: Portrait in Power.* Austin, Tex.: Jenkins, 1973.

Dallas Times Herald. "Bullock Calls John Hill 'S.O.B.' after Speech." April 7, 1978.

———. "Erwin Calls Briscoe's Office Weak." Oct. 25, 1976.

———. "The Sixty-Eighth Legislature." Editorial. Jan. 9, 1983.

Davis, Will. Personal interview. Apr. 26, 2006.

DeBoer, Marvin. *Destiny by Choice: The Inaugural Addresses of the Governors of Texas.* Fayetteville: Univ. of Arkansas Press, 1992.

Dobbs, Ricky F. *Yellow Dogs and Republicans: Allan Shivers and Texas Two-Party Politics.* College Station: Texas A&M Univ. Press, 2005.

Fainter, John. Personal interview. Apr. 26, 2006.

Faulk, John Henry. *The Uncensored John Henry Faulk.* Austin, Tex.: Texas Monthly Press, 1985.

Francis, Jim. Personal interview. June 26, 2006.

Gantt, Fred, Jr. *The Chief Executive in Texas: A Study in Gubernatorial Leadership.* Austin: Univ. of Texas Press, 1964.

Gantt, Fred, Jr., Irving O. Dawson, and Luther Hagard, Jr. *Governing Texas: Documents and Readings.* New York: Crowell, 1974.

Green, George Norris. *The Establishment in Texas Politics: The Primitive Years, 1938–1958.* Westport, Conn.: Greenwood, 1979.

Greene, Robert, and Joost Elffers. *The 48 Laws of Power.* New York: Viking, 1998.

Hammarskjöld, Dag. *Markings.* Trans. Leif Sjöberg and W. H. Auden. New York: Ballantine, 1964.

Helprin, Mark. "Statesmanship and Its Betrayal: The Definition of a Politician." Heroes for a New Era and a New Century Seminar. Hillsdale College, Scottsdale, Ariz. Feb. 7, 1998.

Hickie, Jane. Personal interview. July 29, 2006.

Hobby, Bill. Personal interview. July 25, 2006.

Ivins, Molly. *Who Let the Dogs In?* New York: Random House, 2004.

Ivins, Molly, and Lou Dubose. *Shrub: The Short but Happy Political Life of George W. Bush.* New York: Vintage, 2000.

Jones, Delwin. Personal interview. May 3, 2006.

Jones, Lee. "Charting the Governor's Elusive Path: Is Briscoe's Style a Government in Absentia?" *Dallas Times Herald,* Nov. 23, 1975.

Kinch, Sam. "Clements Gets Silence Treatment." *Dallas Morning News,* Mar. 7, 1979.

Kinch, Sam, and Ben Proctor. *Texas under a Cloud.* Austin, Tex.: Pemberton Press, 1972.

Krajl, Nick. Personal interview. July 5, 2006.

Kuempel, George. "Appointments Battle May Cost Mark White in Long Haul." *Dallas Morning News,* Jan. 4, 1983.

———. "Governor Stands Firm after Override." *Dallas Morning News,* May 18, 1979.

Laney, Pete. Personal interview. Apr. 26, 2006.

Lewis, Gib. Personal interview. July 28, 2006.

Martin, Jack. Personal interview. July 28, 2006.

McDonald, Archie P. *On This Day of New Beginnings: Selected Inaugural Addresses of Texas Governors.* Austin: Texas State Library, 1979.

McKinney, Mike. Personal interview. Apr. 25, 2006.

McNeely, Dave. "Subdued Legislature Regarded as Efficient." *Austin American-Statesman,* May 31, 1983. Austin: Texas State Archives.

Mitchell, E. W: *The Revenge of the Bush Dynasty.* New York: Hyperion, 2000.

Mobley, John. Personal interview. May 2, 2006.

Montgomery, Dave. "Briscoe Appears Unbeatable." *Dallas Times Herald,* Nov. 1, 1973.

———. "Briscoe So-So in his First Crucial Test." *Dallas Times Herald,* June 3, 1973.

———. "Texas First Lady 'Hurt' by Hefty Influence Talk." *Dallas Times Herald,* July 8, 1973.

Morris, Celia. *Storming the Statehouse: Running for Governor with Ann Richards and Dianne Feinstein.* Toronto: Scribner's, 1992.

Murph, Dan. *Texas Giant: The Life of Price Daniel.* Austin: Eakin Press, 2002.

Neustadt, Richard E. *Presidential Power and the Modern Presidents: The Politics of Leadership from Roosevelt to Reagan.* New York: Free Press, 1990.

Nixon Presidential Library and Museum. *Tape 813 Conversations.* http:// Nixon.archives.gov/forresearchers/find/tapes/tape813/tape813.p . . . (accessed Dec. 26, 2007).

Nixon, Richard. *Leaders: Profiles and Reminiscences of Men Who Have Shaped the Modern World.* New York: Warner, 1982.

Perry, Rick. Personal interview. July 6, 2006.

Pittman, H. C. *Inside the Third House.* Austin: Eakin Press, 1992.

Porterfield, Bill. "Gov. Briscoe Has Everything." *Dallas Times Herald,* Aug. 16, 1978.

Powers, Pike. Personal interview. Apr. 21, 2006.

Ramsey, Ross. "Clements: He's Ready to Leave—for Good." *Dallas Times Herald,* Dec. 9, 1990.

Read, Julian. Personal interview. June 20, 2006.

Richards, Ann. Address. Seventy-third Legislature of the State of Texas. *Journal of the House of Representatives,* Jan. 12, 1993.

———. Inaugural Address, Jan. 15, 1991.

———. *Official State Papers.* Austin: Center for American History at the Univ. of Texas at Austin.

———. State of the State Address, Feb. 6, 1991.

Richards, Ann, with Peter Knobler. *Straight from the Heart: My Life in Politics and Other Places.* New York: Simon & Schuster, 1989.

Rodrique, George. "Clements Plays for High Stakes." *D Magazine,* Nov. 1982, 100.

Rogers, Mary Beth. Personal interview. July 3, 2006.

Roosevelt, Theodore. "The Strenuous Life." Speech to the Hamilton Club, Chicago, Apr. 10, 1899.

Rosenthal, Alan. *Governors and Legislatures' Contending Powers.* Washington, D.C.: Eagleton Institute of Politics, Rutgers University / Congressional Quarterly.

Schwartz, Babe. Personal interview. June 13, 2006.

Shropshire, Mike, and Frank Schaefer. *The Thorny Rose of Texas: An Intimate Portrait of Governor Ann Richards.* New York: Birch Lane, 1994.

Smith, Preston. Address. Sixty-first Legislature of the State of Texas. *Journal of the House of Representatives,* Jan. 14, 1969.

———. Address. Sixty-second Legislature of the State of Texas. *Journal of the House of Representatives,* Jan. 12, 1971.

———. First Inaugural Address, Jan. 21, 1969.

———. Second Inaugural Address, Jan. 19, 1971.

———. State of the State Address, Jan. 23, 1969.

Smith, Terral. Personal interview. July 27, 2006.

Smyrl, Vivian Elizabeth. "Permanent University Fund." *The Handbook of Texas Online*. Texas State Historical Association. http://www.tsha.utexas .edu/handbook/online/articles/PP/khp2.html (accessed June 26, 2007).

Spellings, Robert. Personal interview. July 10, 2006.

Stone, Ron. "August 2, 1973." *Book of Texas Days*. [Online. Texas Reference Center database.] Austin, Tex.: Eakin Press, 1984.

Stromberger, Ernie. Personal interview. May 2, 2006.

Temple, Larry. Personal interview. May 1, 2006.

Tolleson-Rinehart, Sue. *Claytie and the Lady: Ann Richards, Gender, and Politics in Texas*. Austin: Univ. of Texas Press, 1994.

Toomey, Mike. Personal interview. Apr. 20, 2006.

Welch, June Rayfield. *The Texas Governor*. Dallas: GLA Press, 1977.

White, Mark. Address. Sixty-eighth Legislature of the State of Texas. *Journal of the House of Representatives,* Jan. 11, 1983.

———. Address. Sixty-ninth Legislature of the State of Texas. *Journal of the House of Representatives,* Jan. 8, 1985.

———. Address. Seventieth Legislature of State of Texas. *Journal of the House of Representatives,* Jan. 13, 1987.

———. Inaugural Address, Jan. 18, 1983.

———. *January 1983–January 1987: A Retrospective*. Austin: State of Texas, 1987.

———. Legislative Accomplishments Press Conference. Austin: Texas State Archives Holdings, June 1, 1983.

———. *Official State Papers*. Austin: Texas State Archives.

———. Personal interview. July 25, 2006.

INDEX

Numbers in italics refer to photographs.

Andrews, Mike, 108
Armstrong, Bob, 66
Armstrong, Tobin, 54, 81
Athens, Texas, 67
Attlesey, Sam, 54, 81
Austin, Texas, 58, 70, 91, 92
Austin American-Statesman, 74, 76, 85, 92, 110

Baker, James, 63
Barnes, Ben
    campaign for governor, 40
    and John Connally, 12, 18–19, 23, 37–38
    ouster from office, 36–37
    and Preston Smith, 23, 25–26
    and Sharpstown scandal, 32, 36–39, 41
Barta, Carolyn, 63, 64, 69
Bashur, Reggie, 65–66, 82, 84, 85, 116–117, 136
Bass, Rita. *See* Clements, Rita Bass
Bay of Campeche, 64
Bell, David, 28–29
Bentsen, Lloyd, 12, 68, 108
Beschloss, Michael, 9
Bomer, Elton, 121, 122, 123, 136
Bonner, Cathy, 101, 105–106, 115–116
Book of Texas Days, The (Stone), 33
Braecklein, Bill, 144n25
Bright, Bum, 81
Brill, Idanell. *See* Connally, Nellie

Briscoe, Dolph, *34*
    accomplishments, 43
    background, 35
    campaigns for governor, 24, 35
    goals for first term, 41–42
    and John Connally, 12, 40
    and John Hill, 44, 49–50, 138
    reelection campaign, 44, 49–50
    tax policy, 41, 43–44
    weakness, image of, 42–43, 134
    wife's influence on, 42
    work habits, 42–43
Briscoe, Janie, *34*, 42, 51
British Broadcasting Company (BBC), 95
Brown Brothers Harriman, 115
budget appropriations, 3, 6, 16, 29, 125, 129. *See also under specific governors*
Bullock, Bob, 79, *103*
    and Ann Richards, 111, 118, 138
    campaign for governor, 72
    and George W. Bush, 119, 124
    and John Hill, 44
    and Mark White, 63, 72
    and Preston Smith, 27
bully pulpit, 6
Burka, Paul, 3, 20, 47, 63, 74, 76–77, 107, 109, 116, 132, 134
Bush, Barbara, 115
Bush, George H. W., 48, 55, 67, *86*, 143n9
Bush, George W., *114*, *120*, 136
    and budget appropriation, 3, 124, 126
    campaign strategy, 4, 118

congressional campaign, 81
decisiveness, 123, 136
legislative agenda, 119–120
and legislators, 119–121, 134
lessons learned, 125
and Patients' Protection Act, 121–122
and Pete Laney, 124–125, 126
and population growth, 116
presidential campaign, 126
tax reform, 124–125, 126
Bush, Laura, *114*
Bush, Samuel, 115

campaign finance, 13, 47, 49, 68, 70, 84,
     98, 100
Carr, Waggoner, 13, 24, 67
Carter, Jimmy, 47, 55
Carter, Rosalynn, *65*
Catarina Ranch (Uvalde), 12, 35, 44. *See
     also* Briscoe, Dolph
Chapman, Jim, 108
Chavez, Norma, 123–124
Chicken Ranch, 33
Churchill, Winston, 4
Cisneros, Henry, 108
Clayton, Bill, 56, 70
clemency, 6–7
Clements, Rita Bass, *46, 48, 49, 50,* 81
Clements, William P., *46, 80, 86*
   appointments, 55, 56, 57
   background, 47–48
   and Bay of Campeche oil spill, 64–66
   campaign tactics (first term), 49–50
   campaign tactics (second term),
        67–68, 82, 84
   disapproval rating, 86
   goals for first term, 51
   and Governor Clements Committee, 55
   and John Connally, 48, 51, 67
   and legislators, 52–53, 56–57, 86–87,
        134
   and Mark White, 54, 57, 59, 63–65,
        81, 138
personality, 47, 68, 77, 137
and play-for-pay scandal, 85–86
and Richard Nixon, 48
and Ronald Reagan, 55, 67
state workers, relations with, 52–53
successes and failures, 52, 54, 57–58,
     87, 137
task forces, 56
Taxpayer Bill of Rights, 51–52, 54
vetoes, 52, 54, 123
and voters' shift to Republican, 54–56
wife's involvement, 49, 81
Clinton, Bill, 91, 108, 109
colonias, 103, 147n32
Committee on Education beyond the
     High School, 14, 19
Committee to Re-elect the President, 36;
     Texas chapter, 48
Connally, John, 10, *18*
   and assassination of JFK, 16–17
   and budget appropriation, 3
   campaign spending, 13
   campaign tactics, 12–13
   and education reform, 14–16, 19
   goals for first term, 12, 13, 14–16
   goals for second term, 19–20
   goals for third term, 20
   In History's Shadow, 89, 129
   and legislators, 4, 17–19, 129, 134
   and Lyndon B. Johnson, 11, 15, 17
   and media, 11, 15
   "midnight appointments," 70
   personal background, 11
   physical characteristics, 17
   and Richard Nixon, 37, 39–40, 48
   State of the State addresses, 13, 16, 19
   tax bills, 16
   and University of Texas Board of
        Regents, 70–71
   and William P. Clements, 48, 51,
        67, 70
Connally, Nellie, 11, *18,* 20
constitution (Texas), 5, 7, 20, 43, 44

Cox, Frank, 65
Cox, Jack, 13
Crichton, Jack, 17
Cryer, Bill, 101
Cutright, John, 93

Dallas, Texas, 17, 29, 69, 82, 100
Dallas Times Herald, 27, 42, 43, 67, 90, 97, 141n13
Daniel, Price Jr., 13, 20, 23, 63
Davis, Morgan, 15
Davis, Will, 12
Dean, David, 56, 65, 144n28
death penalty, 42, 136
Defense Department research contracts, 14
Democratic National Convention: 1968, 25; 1988, 91
Democratic Party (national), 12, 31, 36, 37, 94
Democratic Party (Texas), 37, 38–40, 70, 71, 94, 106, 115–116, 120
Denton, Lane, 93
Department of Defense (U.S.), 48
Doggett, Lloyd, 70
Dubose, Lou, 61

Earle, Ronnie, 92
economy (of Texas), 3, 15
education reform. *See under specific governors*
Eggers, Paul, 25
Elffers, Joost, 135, 138
El Paso Utility Board, 74
Engler, John, 124
Erwin, Frank, 12, 43
Evans, Roy, 23

Fainter, John, 105, 118
Farabee, Ray, 53, 76
Farenthold, Sissy, 39, 41
Faulk, John Henry, 21; *The Uncensored John Henry Faulk*, 45

federal research grants, 12
Ferguson, James "Pa," 7, 146n2
Ferguson, Miriam "Ma," 84, 146n2
Film and Arts Commission, 104
Fine Arts Commission, 19, 20
Flournoy, Jim, 33
Ford, Gerald, 49, 51, 55
Formby, Marshall, 13
Fort Worth Star-Telegram, 12, 83
Foundation for Women's Resources, 105
Francis, Jim, 47, 50, 51, 54–55, 56, 80, 81

Garner, John Nance, 35
General Motors, 105
Gonzales, Alberto, 123
Goulet, Robert, 26
governor (Texas)
    benefits of office, 131
    ideal qualities of, 3–5, 7–8, 41, 100, 132, 133–139
    legislature, relationship to, 4–6, 129, 132–134, 135
    luck, role of, 138
    and media attention, 131–132
    powers of, 3, 5–7, 8, 132–133; appointment, 7; clemency, 5, 6–7; limits to, 5, 132–133, 134; military, 5, 7; veto, 5, 6
    rivalries, role of, 138
    shift from Democratic to Republican, 47, 54
    term of, 20, 23–24, 43, 52, 126
    See also specific governors
Governor's Mansion, 58, 87, 131
Gramm, Phil, 56, 144n26
Granberry, Jim, 43
Greene, Robert, 135, 138
Grover, Henry, 39
Guerrero, Lena, 106–108

Haldeman, Bob, 40
Hance, Kent, 81, 87

Hannah, John, 108
Hardeman, Dorsey, 28
Harding, Warren G., 92–93
Hargett, Ed, 81
Hawkins, Albert, 123
Hickie, Jane, 92, 94, 95, 96, 98, 100,
    101, 107–108, 109, 110, 117, 136
Higher Education Coordinating Board,
    19, 20. *See also* Connally, John:
    education reform
Hightower, Jim, *69*
Hill, John
    as attorney general, 63
    campaign for governor, 24–25, 44, 47,
        49–50, 51, 138
Hobby, Paul, 108
Hobby, William P., ix, 108
    and Bill Clements, 53–54, 56, 137
    and Dolph Briscoe, 41, 137
    as Legislative Budget Board chairman,
        53, 71
    as lieutenant governor, 37, 53–54, 68
Hoover, Herbert, 115
Houston, Texas, 31, 69, 82, 94
Houston Chronicle, 97
Hughes, Karen, 118, 123
Humphrey, Hubert, 25
Hunt, Albert, 68
Hutchison, Kay Bailey, 109
Hutchison, Ray, 49

Industrial Accident Board, 28–29
In History's Shadow (Connally), 89, 129
interest groups, 6
Internal Revenue Service, 37
Ivins, Molly, 119; *Shrub: The Short but
    Happy Political Life of George W.
    Bush*, 61

Jackson, Lee, 52
Johnson, Clay, 123
Johnson, Cliff, 87
Johnson, Lyndon B., 11, 15, 36

Jones, Delwin, 28
Jones, Garth, 25
Jones, Grant, 53
Jones, Lee, 42
Jonsson, John Erik, 15
Jordan, Barbara, 94, 102, 108
Justice, William Wayne, 57
Justice Department, 37

Kennedy, Edward, 144–145n13
Kennedy, John F., 9, 10, 16, 58
Kennerly, T. E., 20
Kirk, Paul, 94
Kissinger, Henry, 134
Kopechne, Mary Jo, 144–145n13
Krajl, Nick, 17
Krueger, Bob, 108–109

Laney, Pete, 52, 119, 124–125, 126–127,
    132
Leedom, John, 144n25
legislature (Texas), 6, 129, 132–133. *See
    also under specific governors*
Lewis, Gib, 137
line-item veto, 6, 16, 29–30, 54, 57,
lobbyists, 42, 71, 100, 121, 125, 126
Locke, Eugene, 12, 23, 24
Loeffler, Tom, 81, 82, 87
Lubbock, Texas, 23, 27, 30

mandamus proceedings, 5
Mann, Gerald, 67
martial law, 5
Martin, Jack, 101, 106, 107, 108, 109,
    117, 118, 134, 137
Mattox, Jim, 95–97
Mauro, Garry, 119
McCall Publishing Company, 115
McKinney, Mike, 29, 30, 32, 101–102,
    132–133
McLendon, Gordon, 24, 142n8
McMahan, Vance, 121, 123
McNeely, Dave, 74, 85, 110–111

media coverage, 11, 15, 40, 74, 131–132, 135
Michener, James, 58–59; *Texas,* 59
Microelectronics and Computer Technology Corporation (MCC), 75, 145n34
"midnight appointments," 70
Milton, Edna, 33
Mitchell, John, 36, 37–38, 40
Mitsubishi, 83
Mobley, John, 18
Montgomery, Dave, 42, 43
Morehead, Richard, 17
Mutscher, Gus, 31–32, 38

Napoleon, 4
National Bankers Life Insurance Company, 31
National Women's Educational Fund, 91
Neustadt, Richard, 8
New York Central Railway, 11
Nietzsche, 4
Nixon, Richard, 3, 25, 36, 37–38, 39–40, 48
no-pass/no-play provision, 61, 75, 83

O'Daniel, Pat, 24
O'Donnell, Peter, 48
Office of Economic Development, 16

Pardons and Paroles Board, 6
Patients' Protection Act, 121
Pentagon, 48
Permanent University Fund, 145n30
Perot, H. Ross, 56, 61, 72, 118
Pierce, Franklin, 115
pork-barrel politics, 30
Porterfield, Bill, 42
Powers, Pike, 68, 70, 74, 82, 83, 136
Presidential Courage (Beschloss), 9
President's Advisory Committee for Women, 91
Prince Charles, 73

Public Utility Commission, 67–68, 73–74, 75

Queen Elizabeth II, 103, 115
quo warranto proceedings, 5

Rains, Jack, 69
Read, Julian, 12, 13
Reagan, Ronald, 51, 55, 56
Republican Party: of Texas, 48, 49, 109, 118
Richards, Ann, 90, 99
    accomplishments, 104–105, 111, 137
    alcoholism, concerns about, 93, 95
    appointments, 106–107
    and Bob Bullock, 118, 138
    campaign finance, 93, 100
    campaign tactics, negative, 96–97
    as county commissioner, 91
    and Democratic party, 115–116, 134–135
    environmental policy, 102–103
    goals as governor, 5, 101–102
    insurance reform, 101, 103–104
    and legislators, 103, 104, 134
    personality, 110–111, 135, 137–138
    political leadership, views on, 100–101, 109, 135
    reelection campaign, 116–119
    and "Robin Hood" scheme, 105
    staff, 109, 134–135
    and state agencies, 101–102
    and state lottery, 104
    as state treasurer, 92–94
Richards, David, 147n15
Richardson, Sid, 11
Rogers, Andy, 17
Rogers, John, 93
Rogers, Mary Beth, 5, 92, 101, 117, 118
Roosevelt, Franklin Delano, 115
Roosevelt, Theodore, 113
Rosson, Peggy, 74

Rove, Karl
  and Clayton Williams, 98–99
  and George W. Bush, 118, 123
  and Kent Hance, 81
  and William P. Clements, 51, 56, 57,
    123, 143n9
Ruiz v. Estelle, 57
Rumsfeld, Donald, 49

Sadler, Paul, 148n29
San Angelo, Texas, 83
Schmitt, Harrison "Jack," 49
Schwartz, Babe, 17, 37, 56, 137
Securities and Exchange Commission,
    31, 37
SEDCO, 64, 81
Select Committee on Public Educa-
    tion, 72
sesquicentennial celebration, 58
Sharp, Frank, 31, 37, 38
Sharp, John, 107, 108
Sharpstown scandal, 31–32, 36–38,
    41, 43
Sharpstown State Bank of Houston. *See*
    Sharpstown scandal
Shelley, Dan, 122
Shepperd, John Ben, 67
Shields, Donald, 85
Shivers, Allan, 5, 31, 67
*Shrub: The Short but Happy Political Life of
    George W. Bush* (Ivins, Dubose), 61
Smith, Forrest, 43
Smith, Preston, 22, 26
  campaign for first term, 23–25
  campaigns for reelection, 39, 49
  failures of first term, 28
  and inaugural ball preparations,
    25–26
  and John Connally, 20, 23–24
  lack of vision, 27, 30
  and legislature, 28, 135
  as lieutenant governor, 13, 16, 28
  pet ("pork-barrel") projects, 30
  and Sharpstown scandal, 31–32, 36
  State of the State address, 27
  vetoes, 28, 29, 31
  vindictiveness, 29
Smith, Terral, 122–124
Southeastern Drilling Company, 48. *See
    also* Clements, William P.
Southern Methodist University, 85
Southwestern Bell Corporation (SBC),
    105–106, 147n36
special elections, 5, 56
special sessions, 5, 6, 28, 72, 75, 76,
Spellings, Robert, 117
staff, governor's, 5, 28, 44, 96, 109, 131,
    134–135
State Board of Insurance, 104
State Conservatorship Board, 104
State of the State address, 5–6. *See also
    under specific governors*
stereotype (of Texas), 20
Sterling, Ross, 35
Stone, Ron, 33
Strauss, Robert, 12
"Strenuous Life, The" (Theodore Roos-
    evelt speech), 113
Stromberger, Ernie, 15, 27, 30, 31

Tarrance, Lance, 82
Tate, Dr. Willis, 56
tax reform. *See under specific governors*
Temple, Buddy, 66
Temple, Larry, 14, 19, 71
Texans for Richard Nixon, 48
Texas (Michener), 59
Texas Air Control Board, 103
Texas A&M University, 70, 73, 82,
    145n30
Texas Department of Commerce, 104,
    105
Texas Department of Housing and Com-
    munity Affairs, 104
Texas Department of Insurance, 104
Texas Department of Public Safety, 76

Texas Election Bureau, 25
Texas Ethics Commission, 102
Texas Industrial Commission, 75
Texas Medical Association, 121
Texas Monthly, 20, 51, 109
Texas National Guard, 7
Texas Natural Resource Conservation
    Commission (TNRCC), 103
Texas Railroad Commission, 66, 87, 107
Texas Technical College. *See* Texas Tech
    University
Texas Tech University, 29–30, 135
Texas Tourist Development Agency, 16
Texas 2000, 58
Texas Water Commission, 103
Texas Youth Council, 43
Tomlin, Lily, 94, 97
Toomey, Mike, 51
Tower, John, 36
Tunnell, Byron, 13, 16, 18–19

Uncensored John Henry Faulk, The
    (Faulk), 45
University of Texas, 11, 14, 30, 47, 59,
    70, 73, 87, 135, 145n30
University of Texas at Dallas, 29, 30
Uvalde, Texas, 35

Walker, George Herbert, 115
Walker, Major General Edwin, 13
Wall Street Journal, 68
Watergate scandal, 43
Weld, William, 124

Whitacre, Edward, 147n36
White, Linda Gale, 66
White, Mark, 5, *62, 65, 69, 73*, 136–137
    accomplishments as governor, 72, 75
    background, 63
    and Bay of Campeche oil spill, 64–66
    campaign for first term, 69
    campaign for second term, 95–97
    and Dolph Briscoe, 40–41
    education reform, 72–73, 75–76
    fiscal challenges, 71–72, 76, 82, 138
    and John Connally, 71
    media, use of, 74
    and Mitsubishi, 83–84
    tax bills, 75–76, 82–83
    and William P. Clements, 54, 57, 59,
        63–65, 81, 138
Whitman, Christine Todd, 124
Williams, Clayton, 4, 147n24
    campaign spending, 100
    public image, 97–98
    weaknesses as candidate, 98–100
Williams, Modesta, 98
Wilson, Will, 13, 37, 38, 67
Woods, Stanley, 20
Wright, Jim, 12

Yarborough, Don, 13, 17, 25
YPF, 48

Zachry, Henry Bartell (Pat), 15
Zimmerman, Julian, 36
Zindler, Marvin, 33

Lightning Source UK Ltd.
Milton Keynes UK
UKOW04f0115061215

264155UK00001B/10/P